DEAR LORD,
THEY WANT ME
TO GIVE THE DEVOTIONS!

John D. Schroeder and Shane Groth

 Abingdon Press

Nashville

DEAR LORD, THEY WANT ME TO GIVE THE DEVOTIONS!

Copyright © 1993 by Abingdon Press

This book is printed on recycled, acid-free paper.

ISBN 0-687-29211-5

00 01 02 — 10 9

Cover Illustration by Charles Cox

MANUFACTURED IN THE UNITED STATES OF AMERICA

CONTENTS

Contents

INTRODUCTION

There was always a predictable silence in our weekly church staff meetings following the question, "Who would like to prepare devotions for next week?" Whether it was an issue of time, knowledge, or feeling uncomfortable leading a group, the topic of devotions seemed to be an unnerving experience, even for pastors.

This book is intended to take the mystery and anxiety out of leading devotions and to increase your confidence in preparing your own devotions.

How to Use This Book

Each devotion has been listed alphabetically by topic so that it can be found quickly and easily. For example, if your church is in the process of adding a new addition to the building or hiring a new pastor or church professional, you might want to use the devotion on "Beginnings" (p. 26). If you've been asked to give a devotion for a large church meeting you might want to pick a devotion on "Celebration" (p. 30), "Unity" (p.103), or "Support" (p. 93). This will allow you to quickly find a devotion appropriate for your needs. The devotional topics in this book are listed in the contents.

You can also use this book for personal devotions or weekly meetings. You can start from the beginning and use one devotion per week. With over 50 devotions, this book will cover a year of meetings.

The Purpose of a Devotion

Much of the confusion and fear of leading a devotion comes from not understanding what the true purpose of a devotion is. The purpose of a devotion is to:

- Show how your faith has been helpful for you;
- Connect the Bible with daily life;

- Build rapport with others (group building);
- Celebrate/rejoice how God has worked in your life or the life of the community (church, nation, or world);
- Raise an issue or faith concern that needs to be addressed;
- Build up the community of faith with a word of encouragement.

You'll notice that sharing theological expertise is *not* the purpose of a devotion. You need not have an advanced degree in theology or be a pastor to share a meaningful devotion. A devotion from the heart—sharing what is personally important to you at the time—is much more appreciated and uplifting than a brief Bible study. The main purpose of a devotion is to share how God has been part of the struggles and joys you experience in your daily walk of faith.

How to Personalize Devotions

Each of the devotions in this book can be read just as they are for personal or group use. The devotions can easily be made more personal, however, to meet special circumstances or to more directly fit the needs of the group, church, or committee meeting.

You'll note that each devotion has three basic parts: 1) an opening Bible verse related to the topic; 2) a story, anecdote, or example that pertains to the topic and Bible verse; and 3) ways the Scripture verse relates, challenges, or encourages us in our lives of faith today.

Personalizing the devotion is as simple as substituting any or all of these three basic components. For example, say your group or committee wants to start a new program. You've been thinking about a Bible verse and have decided that the devotion on "Action" (p. 21) is appropriate. To personalize the devotion you could: 1) use the Bible verse you've been thinking of that fits the theme—keeping the rest of the devotion as is; 2) add an example from your own life or the experience of the group where obstacles were overcome with God's help in the past; or 3) make your own connections about how faith and trust in God has worked miracles in the past in your life or the life of the church. Any or all of these three components could be added to make the devotion more personal.

You could also add a prayer at the end of the devotion for inspiration or encouragement. See the section on "How to Pray in Public" that follows.

Creating Your Own Devotion from Scratch

You can prepare your own devotion, one that is not included in this book, by simply using the same three components of our devotions listed above. Keep in mind that if something is interesting or important for you, it will most likely be important for others. The worst that can happen in giving a devotion is that you might have fun sharing something meaningful to you and show others a bit about who you are as a person. Here are the three basic steps:

First: Faith motivator. If possible, begin with a Bible verse that's been on your mind recently. What issues has it raised? Why has this verse been important for you? How has the verse connected with your daily life? What themes has it addressed?

If a Bible verse does not come to mind first, you can start with a theme instead. Think of what you'd like to share—your motivation for the devotion—and choose a Bible verse that addresses this theme and your audience. Is your purpose to inspire, encourage, motivate, or teach? What would you like to share? What do you think would be most helpful for the group with which you're sharing your message? If you've thought of a theme or topic but a Bible verse does not come to mind, use a concordance or topical Bible to help find an appropriate verse.

Second: Faith story. Think of a story, anecdote, or example from your own life that you feel connects or speaks to the topic and Bible verse. What experience from your own life comes to mind when you think of the Bible verse chosen above? Don't sweat over finding an exciting or unique experience—usually the common experiences with which everyone can relate work best.

Third: Faith in action. This is the time to show how your example or story relates, challenges, or encourages people in their lives of faith today. How was God working or speaking to you in that particular situation? How do you think God is working or speaking to your group or church?

Keep in mind that devotions need not be prepared at the last minute. Keep your ears and eyes open for examples, situations, or Scripture that is particularly meaningful for you, and write these down when they happen. Jot down poems that speak to you. Write down how the Spirit has spoken to you through Scripture during your time of prayer or meditation. Ask for a copy of a sermon that challenged you. Save these in a folder for future reference.

How to Pray in Public

You may want to end your devotion with a short prayer. Praying in public is similar to giving a devotion—we pray to share how God is active in our lives today. Prayer in its simplest form is talking with God. It is *not* an occasion to impress others with how religious we are or to show how much we know about the Bible. Nor is prayer a platform to show how eloquently we speak. Prayer in its best form is an expression to God of our feelings, using the words that come to us at the time. (If you do not feel comfortable praying spontaneously, write down your prayer beforehand and simply read it out loud.)

With this in mind—that the best prayer is a prayer from the heart—here are a few suggestions to quickly prepare for praying out loud:

1. Think of the occasion. Is the group gathering for a Bible study? A funeral? A time of thanksgiving? A meal?

2. Are there any special requests important for those gathered together? For example, if you're gathered for a wedding reception dinner, is there a recent death or birth in the family that should be mentioned?

3. Be honest with your feelings. Are you angry, joyful, worried, unsure, or perplexed? Are you at a loss for words? People can relate to feelings more easily than theological jargon.

4. Be thankful. Even in death we are thankful for the gift and promise of eternal life. For what can we give God thanks? How has God been working in your midst?

5. Be brief. Keep your prayer short. People will appreciate your conservation of words.

Prayer options:

6. Ask people to bow their heads for a moment of silence. This way they can personalize their prayers and speak from their own hearts. You can simply end by saying something like, "Lord in heaven, hear our prayers."

7. Ask people in the group to each share one or two words that summarize their prayer to God at the moment. This is nonthreatening and lets the group get involved.

Like anything else, praying out loud becomes easier the more you do it. A good way to begin is to pray out loud when you are alone to get used to your voice and to become comfortable sharing your feelings publicly. Another way to begin is to practice public prayer in a small group such as your family, a Bible study, or church social group.

FOLLOW-UP QUESTIONS

Once you have presented your devotion before the group on the topic of your choice, you may want to continue the discussion of the topic by using one or more follow-up questions. Using questions to start a discussion after your devotion can be valuable in gaining a deeper understanding of issues and feelings related to the topic.

Here are some advantages of utilizing group questions after reading a devotion.

1. *Questions help bring out the viewpoints of others.*

You can discover if your group agreed or disagreed with the viewpoint(s) expressed and see what they have to add to the devotion. If the topic was important enough to be chosen, chances are there are some strong feelings about it that deserve to be expressed.

2. *Group participation makes a devotion more meaningful.*

Listening to a devotion is great, but talking about your feelings on the topic is even better. It gives people a chance to reveal a bit about themselves and learn from the experiences and opinions of others.

3. *Questions make it possible to explore different issues as related to the topic.*

For example, on the topic of love, participants might want to share their thoughts on love as related to friendship, marriage, building deeper relationships, love of God, love of material possessions, and so on.

4. *A discussion can give people the chance to ask questions of themselves and others.*

Even if people don't talk during a discussion, you can be assured there is an internal dialogue enabling people to get in touch with their feelings. When you ask questions, you also give permission for people to talk to others, exchanging thoughts and feelings.

5. *Your questions can be the start of an ongoing dialogue.*

You might think of your discussion session as a warm-up to a related issue or topic during your meeting. You'll find people may refer back to the devotional and/or the post-devotional discussion during and after the meeting. It may spark telephone calls or talks over lunch. You never know what the result can be of a good discussion among friends.

6. *Questions give you the opportunity to personalize issues.*

As the devotional leader, asking questions puts you in a leadership position that allows you to "get personal" with a topic, direct the group towards specific issues, and solicit feedback from those in your group. You may want to personalize by relating the topic to an event at your church, community, or perhaps a headline in your local newspaper.

7. *Questions take the focus off of you and gives it back to the group.*

It is an excellent transition to a meeting or topic. Asking questions acknowledges that there are other people in the room with thoughts and feelings who might want to express themselves.

Tips About Discussions and Questions

1. Questions should be nonthreatening and serve the purpose of starting a dialogue. Avoid questions that simply repeat information from the text (for example, "What did Jesus say?") or questions that can be answered with a yes or no answer.

2. Focus questions on your particular group or issue. For example: "In what way does this text challenge you? How does it challenge our church? What words of encouragement did it offer?"

3. Set a time limit for the discussion and tell your group how much time you want to devote to discussion.

4. If you ask a question and no one responds, give your own thoughts and feelings on the subject. Serve as an example that it is safe to express an opinion.

5. If time permits, ask for other questions on the topic from those in your group.

6. Remember to thank everyone for participating in the discussion.

Where Can You Use Questions?

1. Retreats. Retreats are ideal because often the time allows for extended periods of discussion. You have more time to explore feelings and build on relationships through dialogue.

2. Bible Studies. Match the devotional topic to the Bible lesson. Then, before starting the lesson, use questions to get others to share their thoughts and experiences.

3. Council/Board Meetings. A brief devotion followed by several related questions can set a positive and spiritual tone for a meeting.

4. Teen Gatherings. Teenagers are full of questions and will appreciate the opportunity to focus on a specific topic and exchange ideas.

5. Church Staff Meetings. After meditating on a devotion, members may want to share how it relates to their work in the church environment. Questions give them a starting point.

Devotions

ACTION

But those who hope in the LORD
will renew their strength.
They will soar on wings like eagles;
they will run and not grow weary,
they will walk and not be faint. (Isaiah 40:31)

If you have ever attempted to win a race or some sort of competition, you know how difficult it can be to overcome the obstacles that prevent us from doing our best. To be a champion requires an enormous amount of persistence, and not many people have what it takes to go all the way.

Many years ago, a salesperson dreamed of becoming the sales champion in her organization. At the time, she had never won an award, but that didn't stop her from aspiring to become the best. She vowed that within one year, she would win the top sales award. And she did. In fact, her sales qualified her for three top awards.

When asked what she learned about winning, she said, "I learned more about trying than I learned about winning during the past year. Trying gave me a renewed confidence that I had gotten off my duff and I'd done something about myself. I learned there may be good reasons for not winning, but there are no good excuses for not trying."

Our God is an active God. He wants us to be just as active in our ministry. It is this call to action that is found in Isaiah. Promises of renewed strength, of soaring with wings as eagles, and of running without weariness are words of high energy and action. The verse assures this endurance for all those who wait upon the Lord.

We don't always have control over winning, but God has given us control over our actions. God wants us to try, to make an effort, so that others may be blessed by our works. God wants us to work while others are resting, to listen when people cry to be heard, and to give of ourselves and to take risks when others play it safe. Our words and actions can be powerful evidence of God's love and presence in this world.

There is power in trying and taking risks, and with God's help you can perform miracles as you touch lives. God doesn't give us excuses to sit on the sidelines. Instead, God gives us reasons to get involved and strength to do his will.

The question before us is how we will respond to the work that lies ahead. With wings as eagles we can soar to new heights. All God asks is that we get out of the nest and try our wings.

ASSUMPTIONS

In their fright the women bowed down with their faces to the ground, but the men said to them, "Why do you look for the living among the dead?" (Luke 24:5)

At the beginning of his career, master showman P. T. Barnum originated a museum display called "The Happy Family." Barnum featured a lion, tiger, panther, and a baby lamb all in the same cage. His unique collection made newspaper headlines and people flocked to see the exhibit. Although it was a financial hit, Barnum appeared worried.

After the exhibit had been running for several weeks, a friend asked Barnum how everything was going. "Oh, fairly well," the showman replied. "I'm going to make a permanent feature out of it if the supply of lambs holds out!"

Appearances can be deceptive because often things are not as they seem. Appearances based on our observations and expectations can fool us again and again.

Today it takes effort to go beyond appearances to discover the truth, but God has called us to seek the truth in all aspects of our lives.

What assumptions do you make in the following situations?

- You turn on a light switch.
- You lend money to a friend.
- You plan to meet someone for lunch.
- You buy something with a written guarantee.

In each of these situations you have assumptions about the outcome. But it is quite possible that what you assume will bear little resemblance to reality.

Could it be that God wants us to make fewer assumptions in our lives and become better acquainted with the truth? Perhaps that "different" person in church is really a lot like you once you become acquainted. Maybe a family that seems to be doing great has some serious problems and needs help. Could it be that we assume others will pitch in and help at church? And how often do we assume our family knows how much we love them?

Going beyond appearances can alter our perceptions about our church, our faith, and our brothers and sisters in Christ. It does take effort and sometimes a risk on our part, but the results obtained can change lives.

Perhaps we need to be more like the small boy who refuted talk of a painless dentist in the neighborhood. "He's not painless at all," the youngster said. "He put his finger in my mouth and I bit it, and he yelled just like anybody else!" (*Readers' Digest Chuckles & Laughs* [New York: Readers' Digest Press, 1964], p. 12.)

BASICS

Where is the wise man? Where is the scholar? Where is the philosopher of this age? Jews demand miraculous signs and Greeks look for wisdom, but we preach Christ crucified: a stumbling block to Jews and foolishness to Gentiles. (1 Corinthians 1:20a, 22-23)

There's a story told about the world-famous mathematician and physicist, Dr. Albert Einstein, while he was working at the Institute of Scientific Research in Princeton, New Jersey. One Friday afternoon, a cleaning woman arrived at the Institute to prepare the classrooms for the next week. When she came to Dr. Einstein's seminar room, she found, as one might expect, sections of blackboard covered with intricate equations and formulas. Over these, Dr. Einstein had boldly scrawled, "Erase."

There was one section, however, over which he had carefully written "Do not erase." Below it was only this: "2 + 2 = 4."

Søren Kirkegaard, philosopher and theologian, was asked one day how he would best summarize his faith. This religious giant, who had written volumes on the intricacies of the Christian faith, simply said, "Jesus loves me, this I know. For the bible tells me so." How easy it is to forget the basics, and yet, how important they are for the proper foundation. For the apostle Paul it was "Christ crucified"; the message he built his life around.

It's comforting to know that we need not be an Einstein to receive what God has given us. God chooses each of us, just as we are, in the midst of our sins, to receive life in Christ Jesus. God gave his Son for us, so that we might have life. And that is as basic as it gets.

BEGINNINGS

The LORD is my rock, my fortress and my deliverer;
my God is my rock, in whom I take refuge. (Psalm 18:2)

When eccentric multimillionaire William Beckford decided to construct his dream home in 1794, it was the beginning of one of the biggest and most extravagant follies in British construction history.

Beckford's great ambition was to build a huge Gothic "abbey" on his estate, complete with lofty halls and high towers. He began construction of Fonthill Abbey by constructing a wall around his entire estate to prevent others from viewing his project. He then brought in hundreds of men to work around the clock on his future home. An additional four hundred men were later added, hired away from a local church construction project.

When work did not go fast enough, Beckford took over supervision of the project himself. As an incentive to finish on time, Beckford rewarded daily accomplishment with larger and larger rations of liquor. Eventually his workers became drunk and incompetent. At one point he had a four hundred foot tower built so he could see how it looked. He then ordered it torn down.

But Beckford's biggest mistake, as well as the literal downfall of the entire project, was his impatience. Always in a hurry, Beckford saw no need for a proper foundation to be dug. His workers built the huge structure upon the foundation originally meant for a small summer home. Beckford was able to eat a Christmas dinner cooked in the abbey's kitchen, although the kitchen walls collapsed later that day. The main tower fell over six years later in 1800. Gradually, the remaining buildings fell as well. Today, there's not much left of Fonthill Abbey, the impractical fantasy of William Beckford.

The importance of a firm foundation is just as vital today, not only in buildings but also in programs, planning, leadership, fund raising, and the many ministries of the contemporary Christian church. Without the right start, time and events can topple anything we construct. Familiar hymns like "The Church's One Foundation" and "Built on a

Rock" remind us that unless we build our lives, our programs, and our congregation on the rock of Christ, what we do will fail.

As God's leaders, how should we begin to build lasting expressions of God's love? It can be through simple things. It might be showing patience as we begin a task or work with others. Our words and actions can be powerful testimony that Christ is the living architect of our lives. Prayer is also a good foundation for beginning any task.

God has called each of us into service. Let's begin with building a firm foundation, consulting the Master each step of the way.

BELIEVE

Let us hold firmly to the faith we profess. (Hebrews 4:14b)

Wfinal hat if you personally were asked to put in writing a summary of your beliefs and philosophy of life in less than 750 words? About 30 years ago, 100 Americans were asked to do just that. Their thoughts and experiences were shared in a book called *This I Believe* (New York: Simon & Schuster, 1952), edited by Edward R. Murrow. Although long out-of-print, the book is a fascinating account of how people's experiences have shaped their lives, values, and beliefs.

A successful attorney who lost his sight at the age of four wrote, "Life, I believe, asks a continuous series of adjustments to reality. The more readily a person is able to make these adjustments, the more meaningful his private world becomes. The adjustment is never easy. I was bewildered and afraid. But I was lucky. My parents and teachers saw something in me—a potential to live—which I didn't see, and they made me want to fight it out with blindness. The hardest lesson I had to learn was to believe in myself."

Another person wrote, "I believe there is no escape from the rule that we must do many, many little things to accomplish even just one big thing. This gives me patience when I need it the most. And then I believe in having the courage to be myself. Or perhaps I should say, to be honest with myself."

A taxi driver recalled the time he found an emerald ring in his cab. "I remembered helping a lady with a lot of bundles that day, so I went back to where I had dropped her off. It took me almost two days to track her down. I didn't get as much as a thank you. Still, it felt good because I had done what was right. In fact, I believe I felt better than she did."

Through many of the essays, the writers express their belief in God, and although it is not a religious book, it certainly shows how God works in people's lives. It illustrates how God cares about people, through people. And what we believe comes through our good and bad experiences with God's people.

Beliefs change over the years. They grow as we grow. But perhaps what matters most is that we live our beliefs as we touch the lives of others and as others touch us. God has created us with the capacity to believe, and it is a precious gift that works best when it is used.

CELEBRATION

The father said to his servants . . . "let's have a feast and celebrate. For this son of mine was dead and is alive again; he was lost and is found." So they began to celebrate. (Luke 15:22-24)

The boy lagged a few steps behind his hurried mother. Her impatient encouragement to hurry up seemed to fall on deaf ears. The boy stared down at his candy, so engrossed that he stopped walking. "Would you like strawberry-banana, or raspberry?" he asked his mother as though it were the most important question in the world.

"Come on, hurry up!" was her only reply.

We live in a strawberry-banana world. There are exciting choices, opportunities, and flavors to enhance our world and add simple pleasures to our lives. More often than not, however, many of us rush past these moments of enjoyment to get on with life. In the process, we miss the very life we seek.

In the well-known parable of the prodigal son, the lost son returns home to the loving embrace of his father. His father does not ask for a confession; he does not ask if his son is truly remorseful for throwing away the family inheritance. What does he do? He celebrates! He gives his son a robe, a symbol of honorable reinstatement. He gives him a ring, a symbol of family authority. He gives him sandals, which elevates him above the status of a slave, for slaves went barefoot. He kills the calf saved only for the most special occasion. The wise father quickly sums up the situation and knows it is time to celebrate, for the lost has returned.

The older son, however, the one who stayed home and did all that his father asked, refuses in this way only—he will not celebrate. He will rejoice neither in the father's love nor God's forgiveness. He is so caught up with being miserable that he misses his chance to celebrate! How much God wants us to celebrate. How much God desires our joy. God rejoices in the one lost sinner who returns home. God relishes in extending and lavishing his grace upon us. God knows how to throw a party! It is not enough for God to celebrate alone, either. God gives all the angels in heaven party horns to join in when the one who was lost returns home.

God's first order of business for each of us is to celebrate. We have been chosen by God from the beginning of the world! The creator of the universe—the one who has defeated sin, death, and the devil—has called us into an intimate relationship. God has created us simply so that God might love us, and we might love God. How can we do anything but celebrate? So go ahead, get out the party horns. We were lost, but now are found!

CHANGE

And we know that in all things God works for the good of those who love him, who have been called according to his purpose. (Romans 8:28)

$\mathbf{A}$re you uneasy about your changing world? Chances are you are not alone. Endings and beginnings are tough for most people. It often seems we are going through a period of adjustment whether we like it or not.

But just like the question, "Is the glass half full or half empty?" it's hard to tell the difference from endings and beginnings. Although most people may prefer the comfort of their work and relationships staying the same, that would eliminate the growth process that accompanies every transition. The stability and security you cherish may vanish with an ending, but the good news is that when something dies, something else is born.

Martin Luther once said, "I have had many things in my hands, and have lost them all; but whatever I have been able to put in God's hands, I still possess" (*Keep Up Your Courage,* Mary Allette Ayer, ed. [Lothrop, Lee & Shepherd, 1908]). We need to learn to let go of things in order to live with any measure of stability. If anything in this world is impossible, it is the effort of attempting to stop endings and beginnings.

To let go and live means to allow some doors to close so new ones may open. Like the saying goes, God does open a window when he closes a door. That can be tough to see sometimes, but if you look back at your life, chances are you can see the hand of God in each and every change. God wants us to remember and cherish the past without clinging to it. We can't go back . . . only forward. Our past, truly, is not our potential.

So as much as we all would like things to stay comfortable and just as they are, we need not fear change because our God is the God of our past, present, and future. Change is part of God's plan for us to grow and do the work God wants us to do while we are alive on this planet.

As our world continues to change, let's remember that to let go of the past allows us to claim the bright future God has waiting for us. And that makes it all worthwhile.

CLAIMED

So do not be ashamed to testify about our Lord . . . who has saved us and called us to a holy life—not because of anything we have done but because of his own purpose and grace. (2 Timothy 1:8a, 9)

The motions are awkward and sporadic. Tiny arms, like windmills, go in one direction and then the next. Head and legs drop and jerk as though the rest of the body has nothing to say about it.

Who is ever ready for the responsibility or claim of a newborn child? Who is ever fully prepared for the ways an infant changes life? Who would suspect it means being catapulted into a new time warp, where hours are set by feedings and diaper changes rather than the hands on a clock? And who can ignore that this new life needs parents to survive?

It matters little whether the child deserves it or not; the very fact that she is living and breathing makes a claim on the parents to love her. And they will love her, one hopes, even though the reasons for such love sink far deeper than the comprehension. In fact, whether the newborn deserves such love or whether the parents deserve such love doesn't seem to fit into the equation—the parents love her because she is theirs, and that is enough.

One wonders if it is enough elsewhere. We stand in line impatiently, or meet someone new for the first time, and our minds fill with silly thoughts like, Does this person deserve my kindness? Or, Is this someone I should like? And then our minds play table tennis with the yeas and nays of such desperateness. Is it not enough that they are there, and they are part of the larger human family, that we respect and accept and love them? Is that not a claim they put on us?

And what about God? Does not God in fact put a claim on us through the creation? Does not the Creator fashion us before we exist? What is the image of God if it is not the stamp of the Almighty itself? Does not God create us to care for and complete a love relationship with us? And so we, too, are claimed, claimed by the love of God that will not let us go.

Still, one wonders if it is enough. We search for love elsewhere, trying to justify our existence through our work and actions. And while they may be honorable, they are not necessary. Nor are they enough.

God's love is enough. It must be enough if we are to live and glory in the freedom such love brings. God calls us as children and gives us life through Jesus Christ. And though we may accept it kicking and screaming, in the end it is the only claim that gives us life. And that is enough.

COMMUNITY

As God has said: "I will live with them and walk among them, and I will be their God, and they will be my people." (2 Corinthians 6:16b).

The cardboard boxes stacked four and five high in the garage told a story; packed inside were the feelings, faces, and memories of past places and past events. The family was moving. But they were not only moving things, they were moving memories and traditions. Their neighborhood, their subset of the earth, their piece of the universe, would be changing. They would be moving away from friends and neighbors and shared concerns and familiarity. They were leaving behind their community and the feeling of being grounded in a life and place larger than themselves.

A teenage boy moved away from his hometown. As he wrote about his new situation he told friends, "The place is fine. But I don't have anybody out here who cares about me." There was no community, no place where he could sink roots to gain nourishment and vitality.

A teenage girl, when asked about returning to school, confided that there was nothing to return for. In fact, there was nothing to live for anymore. "What is it that keeps you going, then?" a friend asked. "Someone to talk to," she said simply. And there it was again. Community. The thread of caring that separates life from death. We are creatures who die in isolation.

As Christians we are people who have been created in community. We do not live our faith only as individuals, but as the body of believers. The healing, caring, and forgiving that give our faith meaning must happen with more than just ourselves. Was it not another person who made your faith meaningful?

It is the body of faith that nourishes and sustains us in times of difficulty. It is the Church that reminds us our life is not simply our own. We live in community, among the communion of saints. That is our creed. And that, too, is our hope. For God loved the world, the community, so much, that he gave his only Son to die for us—for all of us.

CONFUSION

My grace is sufficient for you, for my power is made perfect in weakness.
(2 Corinthians 12:9)

When two-year-old Hannah went trick-or-treating for the first time it was a harrowing experience for her, even though her father was right by her side.

At the first house they went to, a woman came to the door dressed as a ghost and said, "Boo!" Hannah quickly had both hands glued over her eyes and turned to her father for protection. With some difficulty she was finally convinced to accept some candy, but she did it with great reluctance.

After the first house she wanted to go home. Her father couldn't understand why until she asked, "Is someone going to scare me at every house I go to?"

Unfortunately, confusion is not limited to young children. It is amazing how confusion and misunderstandings "haunt" all of us through our lives. It is an ever-present challenge. Misunderstandings occur at home, at work, while driving, at church, and at social gatherings. And if you look in the Bible, Christ's disciples were confused at times, even though Jesus was with them.

Although coping with confusion can be like trying to slam a swinging door, God encourages us to seek the truth. God's grace is sufficient. God's power is made perfect in our weakness. So even though we may not understand life, we can go to God, who has answers for our confusing world.

When you get perplexed and don't know where to turn, it is always comforting to read or remember the promises of God knowing that God is in control. There is no detail in life that escapes God's watchful eye. His power is sufficient for all our most baffling problems.

Coping with confusion is also eased by learning you don't have to understand everything in life. In fact, there are many things you'll never understand as long as you live. But that's all right. It helps us depend more on God.

Once we realize that confusion is part of human nature that we all share (and even cause) from time to time, misunderstandings can be easier to take. They will always be around, but God has given us the resources to handle them.

CRITICISM

That is why, for Christ's sake, I delight in weaknesses, in insults, in hardships, in persecutions, in difficulties. For when I am weak, then I am strong. *(2 Corinthians 12:10)*

Y ou are treacherous in private friendship, and a hypocrite in public life . . . the world will be puzzled to decide whether you have abandoned good principles, or whether you ever had any."

These harsh remarks by Thomas Paine were directed at one of the most unpopular presidents ever to serve the United States. Newspapers demanded his resignation and accused him of being power mad. "You are utterly incapable to steer the political ship into the harbor of safety," one editor wrote.

Secretary of State, Thomas Jefferson, resigned in order to fight him. Congress denied him funds to operate the nation and said he was on the brink of causing civil war.

This hated president was George Washington, now known as the Father of Our Country. Only after he left office did the criticism slow down and his popularity start to climb.

Like Washington, President Lincoln had his share of critics and his own special way of handling it. He said, "I do the very best I know how, the very best I can. If the end brings me out right, what is said against me won't amount to anything. If the end brings me out wrong, ten angels swearing I was right will make no difference" (J. M. Braude, ed., *Remarks of Famous People* [New York: Prentice Hall, 1965], p. 28).

Yes, leaders are criticized. It's part of life. And whether we have been the source or recipient of criticism, we know how much it can hurt. Jesus was criticized, even put to death—the ultimate in criticism. Although he was perfect, Jesus wasn't immune from criticism. He had his critics, and he responded with forgiveness.

We also can practice forgiveness when our words or actions are brought into question. And we can use criticism as a starting point for implementing productive change in our lives. Criticism need not destroy us; it can transform us.

"He has a right to criticize who has a heart to help," wrote Lincoln. When it comes to giving, it's what is in our heart that's most important in the sight of God. Our intent is the key to whether this force is constructive or destructive. The choice is ours. With God's help we can do what's right.

DEATH

For I am convinced that neither death nor life, neither angels nor demons, neither the present nor the future, nor any powers, neither height nor depth, nor anything else in all creation, will be able to separate us from the love of God that is in Christ Jesus our Lord. (Romans 8:38-39)

The father wanted to explain the concept of death to his three-year-old son because of the recent death of an aunt. The father began by saying that Aunt Janet had died. He then asked his son, "Do you know what death is?"

The father was surprised when the child said he knew, so he asked his son to tell him about death.

"It's what happens when you leave the yard and cross the street by yourself," was the reply.

"Well, no," the father continued slowly. "When someone dies they go to heaven. We won't see Aunt Janet anymore. She's with Jesus, who is also in heaven."

The young boy paused for a moment, then looked intently at his father. "Was Jesus a bad boy? Did he cross the street by himself?"

Obviously the message about the dangers of crossing the road had been well learned.

Making connections about life and death is not an easy task. The reasons and questions surrounding death is not always clear. We struggle and grope for answers.

So often at the time of death the focus seems to be on human actions. We ask ourselves, What else could I have done? What should I have said? If only I had spent more time, if only I had cared a little more, and so on.

In death, our focus instead should be on God's actions. God has defeated death. God has given us another life, more perfect and peaceful than our life on earth. Death is not our defeat—it is God's victory and the beginning of eternal life.

Perhaps we should view death as crossing the road. We go to another place to be with God where there will be no pain or sin or death or struggle. Instead there will be joy and peace and God.

DEVILS

If God is for us, who can be against us? (Romans 8:31)

Some people seem to have a "devil of a time" coping with life. Ever consider it could be the work of a devil? Gandhi, when told the British were devils, replied, "The only devils in this world are those running in our hearts, and that's where our battles ought to be fought." Just as some see devils in the world, Gandhi saw devils within us.

Take the devil of anger, for example. When you are mad at someone, what you are actually doing is allowing that person to enter your life. But when you think about it, is that what you really want? Do you want somebody controlling you? That's why God has given us a release from the devil of anger. There is really no need to be angry at anyone.

Or consider the devil of fear. There are so many fears in life. There is the fear of losing your health or your job. You may be afraid of another person. Some people have a fear of meeting new people, or of even flying on an airplane. Yet with all of these fears, God also provides a release. God's promises to us can stop the devil of fear in its tracks. Faith is a powerful weapon against fear and many of the other devils we face.

There is no limit to devils—emotions, conditions, and feelings that prevent us from being happy, whole, and at peace with God and our world. Negativity is a devil. So are hate, greed, envy, illegal drugs, disease, and poverty. And the truth is they will always be around. We live in a world of devils and the only escape is Christ Jesus, who sets us free from all evils that confront us.

But God not only sets us free from devils, God can use devils for good in our life. Loss becomes gain. Weakness becomes strength. God works wonders in our lives and the lives of others when we turn our devils over to him. The problems we face can be strengthening. What would life be without obstacles that test and challenge us?

There are no easy answers to overcoming the devils we face. We must deal with them one by one, using the resources God has given us. When we use our energy wisely, coupled with prayer and believing the promises of God, our devils don't have a chance. It's because the love of God is stronger, and so are we when the love of God is in us.

EMPOWERING

When they saw him, they worshiped him; but some doubted. Then Jesus came to them and said, "All authority in heaven and on earth has been given to me. Therefore go and make disciples of all nations." (Matthew 28:17-19a)

The day came to life hot and sticky, the kind of sticky that refused to let skin and clothes stay dry. As the volunteers dressed for another day in the Cumberland Mountains of Tennessee, they could feel by the heat of the morning that the mercury would be edging its way toward 100 degrees.

A youth group was attending a week long work camp with the Tennessee Outreach Project. The project was intended to provide home and land improvements for those in need living in two of the surrounding counties. Its task was to help meet the social, spiritual, or physical needs of others. The hope was that if volunteers helped in one area, those people helped would be motivated to do something for themselves in another area. In camp terminology this was known as "empowering others."

Did it work? John Crisp envisioned putting in new glass windows for his house after seeing a new coat of paint applied by one group. Terry Massey said he intended to plow and plant next year on land that had been partially cleared by another Outreach group. Harry Stubblefield, who had a porch added last year through the Project, was now in the process of building his own addition.

Empowering is realizing where the skills and talents of others lie, and then encouraging them to pursue their dreams through their own actions. It's taking a step of faith to challenge and stretch those around us. It's using support and encouragement to aid others in using their God-given gifts. It's taking a risk ourselves that we can make a difference in the lives of others. It's believing that what we do really matters, not only to those around us, but to God and the world. Empowering is what Jesus did when he sent the gift of the Holy Spirit into a handful of people who then turned the world upside down.

Empowering is assisting others so that they might dream dreams and act on them in a realistic and tangible way. As they said in camp, "Give a person a fish, and they can eat for a day. Teach a person how to fish, and they can eat for a lifetime."

EMPTINESS

Why are you downcast, O my soul? (Psalm 42:11a)

Industrialist Albert Nesbitt tells about the time he came face to face with himself and realized there was something quite empty about his life. At the time he was president of a large manufacturing company. By worldly standards, he was successful. But it didn't seem to be adding up to anything.

He writes, "I began to wonder what to do. It occurred to me that I was too wrapped up in my job, to the sacrifice of the basic values of life. It struck me abruptly that I was being quite selfish, that my major interest in people was what they meant to me, what they represented as business contacts or employees, not what I might mean to them."

At the time Nesbitt was having bitter fights with a union. He decided to look at their point of view—and do something about it. He endeavored to apply—literally apply—Christian principles to dealings with employees. The results were remarkable, paying rich dividends in human dignity.

He said, "The actual application of Christian principles changed my life. That feeling of emptiness, into which I was pouring cocktails out of boredom, was filling me up with a purpose: to live a full life with an awareness and an appreciation for other people. It seems to me better to have a little religion and practice it than to think piously and do nothing about it" (*This I Believe* [New York: Simon & Schuster, 1952], p. 127).

When we are feeling empty, when satisfaction seems elusive, it could be a signal that we have lost touch with God who gives us meaning and purpose. Like Nesbitt found, sometimes it takes living our life for others to bring out all the joy, love, and promise God wants us to have in our relationships with him and others.

"What I want is, not to possess religion but to have a religion that shall possess me," writes Charles Kingsley. That's a sure cure for emptiness—Christianity brought to life!

George McDonald says it best. "How often we look upon God as our last and feeblest resource! We go to him because we have nowhere else to go. And then we learn that the storms of life have driven us, not upon the rocks, but into the desired haven."

ENEMIES

"But I tell you who hear me: Love your enemies, do good to those who hate you, bless those who curse you, pray for those who mistreat you. If someone strikes you on one cheek, turn to him the other also." (Luke 6:27-29a)

Just before the Civil War, a young boy wrote in his diary about attending church that day:

> Went to church in the morning, the fernace was all write. Mister Lenard preeched about loving our ennymies, and told every one if he had any angry feeling towards ennyone to go to him and shake hands and see how much better you wood feel.
>
> After church I went up to Micky Gould who was going to fite me behind the school house and said Micky lets be friends. Micky said i can lick you in two minits and i said you aint man enuf and he called me a nockneed puke, and i called him a wall eyed lummix and he gave me a paist in the eye and I gave him a good one in the mouth. We rassled and Mr. Purington pulled us apart and i had Mickys necktie and some of his hair. My father made me go to bed and stay there all afternoon for fiting.
>
> Next time i try to love my ennymy i am going to lick him first. (Henry Shute, *The Real Diary of a Real Boy* [Boston: Everett Press, 1903], pp. 40-42)

As this humorous illustration shows, sometimes loving your enemy isn't all that easy. The writer of the diary was motivated to love and made the attempt, but the results were less than perfect. And perhaps that has a lot to say about human imperfections.

We aren't perfect. At times our intentions are good. We would really like to love our enemies, but matters change when:

> A driver of a car cuts in front of us.
> Someone owes us money and repayment is slow.
> We are criticized unjustly for our actions.
> A person purposefully hurts us.

These are the enemies of today. Usually they are not the type of enemies you physically fight against. Instead they are people who annoy us, are inconsiderate, rude, or don't do things the way we think they should be done. But Christ calls us to love.

What is the solution if we want to be obedient to what Christ commands? Forgiveness. It isn't easy. However, it is an effective strategy for dealing with hurts, anger, and resentment. And it doesn't resolve all our feelings immediately, but it is a necessary beginning.

God does help us love our enemies by empowering us through love. As Christ has forgiven us, we are free to forgive others. That's what loving your enemies is all about.

FAITHFULNESS

"His master replied, 'Well done, good and faithful servant! You have been faithful with a few things; I will put you in charge of many things. Come and share your master's happiness!'" (Matthew 25:23)

Kris, an adult volunteer working with youths, was elated after the Sunday evening gathering. Even though only two people had shown up to participate in the discussion and games, Kris felt good about the rapport she had built with the junior high youths. The night was a success, and the youths asked excitedly about next week's program.

As Kris was leaving, one of the adults from another church function asked how the weekly program had gone.

"Great!" said Kris, "we had a wonderful time."

"How many youths were there?" was the next question.

"Two."

"Hmmm. Oh well. You know, we've just got to get more kids coming to those things. I just can't understand why we can't get more youths involved."

An elated Kris returned home frustrated and dejected. A wonderful evening had been spoiled by someone counting heads, as though success and numbers were synonymous.

God's primary call is not to be successful, but to be faithful.

Jesus told parables to indicate how he felt about numbers and success. In the parable of the talents, the master's response was exactly the same to the two servants who had doubled their money, even though the first servant raised 250 percent more raw capital than the second. Both had been faithful in using the resources available.

In the parable of the sheep and goats, when God separates the people in the last days from the heavenly throne, the question is not, Have you been successful? or How many people have you saved? Rather, the question is, Have you fed the poor, clothed the naked, visited the sick and lonely? In other words, have you been faithful to your call? Again, God calls us to be faithful, not successful.

Numbers simply do not tell the whole story, especially where ministry is concerned. Who can put a value on a changed life?

The Good Shepherd leaves the 99 sheep to look for the one lost sheep because numbers are simply not a priority. We are called, too, to leave the shelter of our safe and familiar flocks so that we might hear the Master say, "Well done my good and faithful servant. You have been faithful with a few things. Come and share your master's happiness!"

FEAR

But the angel said to them, "Do not be afraid. I bring you good news of great joy that will be for all the people." (Luke 2:10)

The six-year-old girl lost her first tooth and called to tell her aunt and uncle about the event. When asked if it had hurt she said proudly, "It didn't hurt a bit. I pulled it out all by myself."

It was an exciting day for the young girl until she laid down in bed with her tooth positioned securely underneath her pillow and began thinking. She knew the Tooth Fairy was supposed to come during the middle of the night, but now she wanted no part of the visitation. "I'm scared," she told her mother as the young girl made periodic sojourns from her bed to the kitchen. "It's you, isn't it Mamma? Are you the Tooth Fairy?"

"It'll be all right," her mother soothed."Everything will be just fine. Now go back to bed."

An older couple prays that they might have the gift of a child. But when an angel of the Lord appears in the Temple with an answer to their prayers, the husband Zechariah is taken aback with fear. "Fear not," is the angel's reply. A newly engaged woman, a virgin by the name of Mary, is startled by the angel Gabriel's greeting of her favored position in the eyes of God. "Fear not," the angel comforts her. A group of shepherds, scraping to make a living in the area around Bethlehem, is suddenly surrounded by the glory of the Lord, and the shepherds are terrified. And the angel says, "Fear not."

In the midst of fear and doubt, in the midst of trembling and uncertainty, spring forth words of assurance and hope. "Fear not, everything will be just fine. The Lord is making sure of it."

Such certainty is the message of the Savior. Something has come to dispel our fears. Something greater than the unknown is here to bring light out of the darkness. Out of our created and subsidized fears of loneliness and uncertainty God says, "Fear not. I am with you until the end of the age."

Fear not. Fear not that your life will pass away, for one has come who has promised you a greater life. Fear not that your days will be spent in solitude without children, for God has sent his son into the world, into your world, to give peace and hope. Fear not that the unknown will suddenly swallow you up and leave you for dead, for Christ has swallowed up death and given us victory over its nasty and enduring shadows.

Fear not, for we have seen and have known the Messiah, Emmanuel, which means "God is with us."

FORGIVENESS

Forgive us our debts, as we also have forgiven our debtors. (Matthew 6:12)

A man and his teenage son were driving through an inner city in the Midwest late one night when the father stopped the car to pick up three young hitchhikers. Once in the car, one of the hitchhikers pulled a gun. The father drove the car into a tree, running away to draw attention from his son who remained in the car, dazed from the impact. As the father fled, he was shot three times. He was killed. The hitchhikers escaped.

A few days after the funeral, the man's wife wrote "an open letter to the three boys that murdered my husband" and gave it to the news media. It read:

> During the past three days my grief and desolation have been eased and comforted by the love and faith of so many wonderful friends and relatives. But, in the midst of all this, and especially in the quiet moments, my thoughts keep turning to you three. You may feel that you are men, but to me you are just boys, like my own sons, and I wonder to whom you are turning for comfort, strength and reassurance.
>
> I suppose I will never know what motivated your actions that night, but if the shots were fired out of sheer panic, my heart aches for you and I wish there were only some way I could help you in what you must be suffering now. If hate made you pull the trigger, I can only pray that you come to know the love of God that fills the heart and leaves no room for hate.
>
> Please, if you see this, find a church someplace where you can be alone; then read this again. Know that God forgives you and that my family and I forgive you—then go out and make something worthwhile of the rest of your lives.
>
> God keep and bless you. (*Minneapolis Star Tribune*)

Forgiveness isn't easy. To be hurt can produce anger, hate, and resentment. And there is the temptation to forgive, but not forget. Yet Christ calls us to unconditional love, to break down the barriers between us, and to become one in Christ.

As Christians, we are to be examples to others of healing broken relationships in this world, one person at a time. And yet, like this woman and her family, we can only begin to forgive others as we focus on God's divine forgiveness for us. May God's mercy move us to forgive as we ourselves have been forgiven.

GENEROSITY

Wisdom brightens a man's face and changes its hard appearance. (Ecclesiastes 8:1b)

In a small western mining town during the 1940s, Wong Hop operated a small cafe and grocery store. He was a generous man and extended credit to everyone, especially the miners who made up most of his business.

When World War II began, the town lost most of its population as the miners were drafted into service. The departing men owed Wong Hop hundreds of dollars at the time and many feared the town's most generous man would go bankrupt. But Wong Hop didn't appear concerned.

The day before the miners left town, Wong Hop held a farewell banquet in the town hall. People encouraged him to use the occasion to ask the miners to pay their debts.

However, as each guest departed, Wong Hop shook hands and pressed a crisp new five dollar bill into each hand. Later, a friend asked him why he gave away money and never talked about the debts.

"It makes my face to shine," replied Wong Hop. If you are lucky, perhaps you know people like Wong Hop, whose appearances radiate with a loving glow. You know them by their kind words, hugs, and willingness to go the extra mile for someone in need. They are the people who can seemingly melt the hardness of our hearts. They brighten each day by giving away gifts of themselves, but never exhausting their treasures.

It's true, wisdom makes us shine. Not the wisdom of the world, as some might think, but "God's secret wisdom" as the apostle Paul phrased it. It is a wisdom accompanied by the Spirit that knows true happiness comes as we give our life in service to others, a wisdom that gives our faces a detectable radiance.

"If you want to be not only successful," said Kenneth McFarland, "but personally happy and permanently successful, then do your job in such a way that, even when you are out of sight, folks will always know which way you went, by the lamps you left behind."

God has given us a mouth to offer appreciation to others, arms to hug, and feet to serve. We shine when we give, no matter how big or small the gift may be.

GIFTS

There are different kinds of gifts, but the same Spirit. There are different kinds of working, but the same God works all of them in all men. (1 Corinthians 12:4, 6)

Have you ever wondered what Jesus did with the gold, frankincense, and myrrh given him by the Magi? Did he ever make use of them, or did his parents simply toss them out?

Many people have probably wondered the same thing about gifts they've given others. "Boy, that sure was a waste of money," we may have caught ourselves saying after someone has all but rejected our gift. Perhaps we should have two responses when we receive gifts. The first could remain a genuine, "Thank you." The second response, this one for a gift we do not appreciate, could be a hearty, "Rest in peace!"

What are the most meaningful gifts we can give to others? One is the gift of self, a gift purchased and wrapped by our Lord and Savior. As the apostle Paul wrote, it is God that works in and through each of us. Other meaningful gifts can be those that bring out the uniqueness of others, gifts that challenge, encourage, and accentuate the variety of characteristics and personalities given to our sisters and brothers in Christ. Such gifts not only fill a need, but more importantly create a need. They create a need for others to use their God-given talents in service to others. They create a need that encourages others to pursue their visions and vocations in the world.

Meaningful gifts could focus on the talents and interests of others. They could be gifts that reflect the character of the individual. They could be gifts that challenge others, that move others out into the wilderness, gifts that allow others to take risks. They could be gifts that tickle and irritate a sense of complacency, gifts that propel others forward with renewed enthusiasm.

The saying still holds true: "We make a living by what we get, but we make a life by what we give."

GRACE

I am not ashamed of the gospel, because it is the power of God for the salvation of everyone who believes: first for the Jew, then for the Gentile. (Romans 1:16)

It was a veteran seminary professor teaching a course on Pastoral Care and Counseling who first mentioned the radical idea. "Secular counseling services can be helpful," he began, "but there's one thing they can't offer—the cross of Jesus Christ."

A pastor fresh out of seminary wondered if it was really true. How could she, simply by being a pastor, offer a privilege that evaded the secular therapists? What did the power of the cross and the forgiveness of sin matter amidst so many other complex problems? Was it really anything different than saying, "Aw, it's all right, I'm okay, you're okay"?

The woman found an answer to her question late one evening. A voice on the other end of the phone stalled and said, "I can't live anymore. I've broken every commandment. I've even killed a person. Can God forgive me, even for that?"

The pastor tried to remain calm as her body shook at the intensity and honesty of the question. Was there indeed forgiveness and grace and salvation for this person? Was it possible to wield such power, to pass on grace so liberally? But that was her call. "Even Moses killed a man," she stammered, "and God chose him to lead the people of Israel into the promised land." She paused, overwhelmed by the possibility. "Yes, God can forgive you even for that," she heard herself say.

The two talked some more and decided to meet that same night. Sitting under a half moon by the side of a local country store, the forgiveness of sins was proclaimed. There was pain, but there was also a release and tears of joy. The cross of Christ broke the dam of welled-up anger, hostility, and self-inflicted punishment that had infected the soul for years. No, the battle wasn't over, not by a long shot, but a new life had been given. A glimmer of hope and healing had been planted by the proclamation of the gospel.

As the pastor drove home through blackened skies and whispering country roads, the face of the veteran seminary professor came into focus. "There's one thing secular therapists can't offer. . . . " She was glad and proud and humbled to be called to share such a message.

That is the message and privilege of every believer; to proclaim God's saving message in Christ. We can proclaim along with the apostle Paul that we are "not ashamed of the gospel, because it is the power of God for the salvation of everyone who believes."

GROWTH

So then, just as you received Christ Jesus as Lord, continue to live in him, rooted and built up in him, strengthened in the faith as you were taught, and overflowing with thankfulness. (Colossians 2:6-7)

M any trees on the shores of Lake Superior jut out and grow on the sheer cliffs and rocky ledges. The long roots, like scouts in search of food and protection, bury themselves in cracks and crevices. The trees grow strong and straight even in solid rock because the roots provide nourishment and support even in the most precarious positions.

The apostle Paul knew that the strength of our faith is not determined by what shows on the outside. The power and persistency and source of our faith is not always displayed to all the world, like the leaves or branches of a tree. Instead, true faith develops in our unseen lives. True faith comes from the roots, from deep inside our hearts. True faith begins in the darkness of our fears and in the shadows of our soul. Our faith, our life in Christ, grows and develops from within. As Paul says, it is "rooted and built up" in Jesus.

A young woman who had just started college wrote a letter to a friend saying, "I think it's kind of neat, and it's so much fun here in college, because unlike high school, no one makes you feel stupid for being smart." She was sensing the joy of having others look beyond the branches and the leaves and to appreciate the heart and roots of who she was as a person.

God isn't concerned with the make-up; God wants to start working with the roots, because in the roots there is life and growth and nourishment. If you cut off the branches of a tree, it can still grow. But if you cut off the roots, cut off the source of growth, it withers and dies.

Be "rooted and built up" in Christ. It's not an easy task. It takes courage to begin in the darkness of our souls to let Christ's light shine in. But it's also deep in the roots that we can believe in a God that can bring healing and life, even in the midst of death and destruction. It's deep in the roots where the movement of the Holy Spirit can begin to make changes. God is waiting to get involved in our lives to give us an abundant life, but God needs room to work. God needs access to the roots so that we can be firmly planted and grounded in the source of all creation and goodness.

"So then, just as you received Christ Jesus as Lord, continue to live in him, rooted and built up in him, strengthened in the faith as you were taught, and overflowing with thankfulness." If we are not rooted and grounded in Jesus Christ, we will wither and die.

GUIDANCE

The LORD is my shepherd, I shall not be in want. (Psalm 23:1)

Walter had three days' work to complete in a day. There were a few things, like an important proposal for work that couldn't wait, and he was feeling the pressure to get it done. He had also felt sick for the last few weeks, however. His body ached and seemed to demand sleep. He made his 7:30 A.M. breakfast meeting, but decided afterward that he had had enough. He called in sick to get some rest.

When he awoke in the afternoon, the pressure to start working began to build. He was overwhelmed with what awaited him. How could he ever get it all done? He was sick, after all, and had just lost another day of work. How was he going to do it?

When the signs of feeling sorry for himself began to show through, Walter decided to pick up the Bible to read a few psalms. For some reason, however, he couldn't stop reading after just a few. He began with Psalm 118 and kept reading, absorbed, until he ended with Psalm 150. Verse after verse told of God's mercy and compassion and unending love for God's people.

As Walter thought about the verses, he realized that the words were for him. God was looking after him. But he was so concerned about himself that he had forgotten about God. If anyone could take care of his work load, God could! So Walter prayed, sharing his powerlessness and trusting in God's guidance. When he finished, the heaviness of his schedule was gone.

Though the task of writing a proposal was still daunting for Walter, he decided to give it a try. An idea popped into his head; and then another; then the whole proposal took shape in a record fifteen minutes! Several hours later he had an acceptable proposal in hand, all done in one-third the usual time. God's message was loud and clear: "Let me take care of your burdens. Look to me for guidance. Let me prove to you that I am the Shepherd who takes care of the sheep."

For Walter, it was another reminder how important it was to let

God be the guide, even when headed into the valley of the shadow of death. God is the one who tends and nurtures us. God is the one who tracks us down when we stray from the path. God is the one who watches and protects us. We need to be the sheep, for only then can we join with the psalmist and say, "The Lord is my shepherd, I shall not be in want."

HAPPINESS

"I tell you the truth, no servant is greater than his master, nor is a messenger greater than the one who sent him. Now that you know these things, you will be blessed if you do them." (John 13:16-17)

It was one of those conversations that spring up around high school reunion time, when comparisons are inevitable, and someone always seems to be making it big on Wall Street or in real estate. "I wonder how Cindy Mork is doing," said the wife to her husband as they drove to the ten year reunion. "I hear she married a wealthy lawyer and is living in a mansion out in California. . . . Wouldn't it be fun to have money like that?"

The question triggered a string of items the couple would buy the minute they had that kind of money—the computers, the cars, the two-story brick colonial house with five bedrooms. They dreamed about other things that would suddenly become necessary for such well-to-do folks, and then sat in silence for a few minutes, thinking. "Do you think we'd be any happier with all that money?" asked the husband. They looked at each other and shook their heads. "Probably not."

A college professor related some of the goals his college students shared with him for their lives after graduation. Happiness was often their life-long ambition.

"Happiness is not a goal," he would share with his students, "something we can obtain through money or hard work. It is a by-product of intentional living. When we live our lives to the fullest, making use of every minute available to us in service to others, we will be happy."

His message was that happiness is not an isolated occurrence found in "things," but rather comes from the way we live. Things alone do not make one happy, whether it be a better sermon, an increase in new members, a new addition, or a more attractive offering envelope. Happiness comes through serving.

Thomas Merton, the great Roman Catholic monk and theologian said, "A happiness that is sought for ourselves alone can never be found; for a happiness that is diminished by being shared is not big enough to make us happy."

HELP

I waited patiently for the LORD;
he turned to me and heard my cry.
He put a new song in my mouth,
a hymn of praise to our God. (Psalm 40:1, 3a)

The wintry winds of Minnesota were picking up. It was getting cold out on the ice of Lake Mille Lacs, but the two fishermen were sitting comfortably inside the fish house. It had been dark several hours now, and the warm glow of the gas stove dwindled to a few flickers of red and orange before it went out completely. "John, I think we've got a problem here. The heater just went out."

Though Perez liked to dabble in the mechanical, bottled gas and matches meant one thing to him—explosion. He tentatively tried to get the heater going again, but it didn't work. Thirty minutes later the temperature inside the house had dropped to nearly freezing. The two men checked their sleeping bags to see if they could make it through the night. "Isn't there someone next door that could help?" John asked. "Well, yea," Perez replied, "but he's been in bed for hours . . . his lights went out right after 5:00 P.M. Do you think we should wake him?"

Since Perez was already dressed in his warmest clothes, he begrudgingly walked over to the neighbor's icehouse and woke him. The neighbor was over in a minute, trying to heal the wounded propane cylinder into pumping out a little heat. Twenty minutes passed with no luck. "Sorry guys," he said, "I think you need a new heater. This one is shot. We really can't do much 'til mornin.'"

Perez and John sat alone in the dark, letting their thoughts get the best of them. Perez decided to go over to the heater once more, to give it one more try. This time, however, he not only had a flashlight in hand, he also had a prayer of help in his heart. The first attempts failed. But then there was a puff, and a chug, and rush of wind, and a flame! The heater was going! They didn't have to freeze after all!!

How long it takes sometimes for us to ask for help, even if our life depends on it! We hesitate, we make excuses, we postpone decisions to get our life back on track. How hard it is to admit we can't do everything by ourselves, especially if we have to admit it to God!

Roberta Bondi, in her book *To Love As God Loves* (Augsburg Fortress, 1987), makes the interesting discovery that the people who recognize their need are the ones who are able to approach Jesus in the Gospels. Those who recognize their need for God are healed. Those who admit their shortcomings are lifted up. Those who admit their sins are forgiven. Those who cry out for help are saved.

As Perez recounted the incident he said, "I hope I don't need to be out on the ice again in a life-threatening situation before I remember to cry out to God for help."

May each of us learn to pray with the psalmist saying:

> In my anguish I cried to the LORD,
>   and he answered by setting me free.
> The LORD is with me; I will not be afraid. (Psalm 118:5-6)

HONESTY

What causes fights and quarrels among you? Don't they come from your desires that battle within you? (James 4:1)

The story is told that when President Grover Cleveland's second child was born, the doctor asked Cleveland to fetch a scale so the baby's weight could be determined.

Cleveland searched throughout the house without success. Finally he remembered he had an old scale in the basement which he had used on his fishing trips. He got it out and brought it upstairs. Carefully the doctor placed the baby on the scale and was amazed to learn that the new-born infant weighed twenty-five pounds.

Perhaps you have already noticed that people sometimes have a tendency to stretch the truth. It happens at work, at home, among friends, and between acquaintances. And it is quite embarrassing when the exaggeration is uncovered.

God has called us to be honest in all that we say and do, but how easy it is to use a "little white lie" for something we think is not that important or where we feel we need to look good in front of others. Whether it is telling the boss how much time you spent on a project at work, or bragging to a friend how large the fish was that you caught, the result is the same. The truth is not in us.

There is an old proverb that says, "The archer that overshoots misses as well as he that falls short." It seems only honesty hits the target.

As the previously quoted verse from James says, it is our desires that are at the root of the problem. Our desire for popularity, acceptance, happiness, love, and other human needs sometimes cause a war to rage within us when honesty and "white lies" come face-to-face. It is usually our self-serving desires that do us in.

What's the answer? A first step can be yielding greater control of our words and actions to God, a process that strengthens us as we grow in faith over a lifetime. And perhaps we should also take a look at our own self-esteem for the reasons why we need to ever exaggerate in the first place. When we accept ourselves as the good children of God that God created us to be, this can lessen our need to prove things to others or alter the truth.

As we continue to learn that God's amazing grace is sufficient for us in all areas of life, we can learn to speak more in truth and less in half-truths.

Remember, when truth is in your way, chances are you are on the wrong road.

HOPE

Why are you downcast, O my soul?
Why so disturbed within me?
Put your hope in God,
for I will yet praise him,
my Savior and my God. (Psalm 42:11)

The rumblings inside of Michelle's soul were a clear indication that something was wrong. Certainly her soul was disturbed within her. The joy of daily tasks had turned into moments of frustration. Her heart, rather than absorbing the excitement of outside activity and challenges, hardened from the struggle within.

It was the new youth worker she was trying to incorporate into the church's youth program. For her, such a person was an integral part of the church's ministry, but there were simply no funds available. What should she do?

Her first reaction was to fight for the cause. She told the church council the reasons they needed such a person. She gave facts and figures to support her case. She piled up evidence and volunteer support to buttress her arguments. People could see the obvious need for such a person, but the bottom line was money. Michelle felt that it was her against them.

The battle continued, both within her and outside her. But she needed no enemies, for she created her own, more vicious and deadly than any that existed elsewhere. Doubt, self-persecution, self-pity, and misunderstanding were their names. Yes, her soul was certainly disturbed and disquieted within her, even though like the psalmist she searched for God's presence and guidance. Was she not looking in the right place?

As Michelle continued to read daily from Scripture, it was the psalmist who revealed the self-inflicted plight of her struggle. She was looking for God, yes, but looking for God to be on her side. She was looking for a god who would nod a head of approval with her. But in doing so she had not only set up a puppet god, but had missed the hope as well. She had missed the hope of waiting for God to act in God's time and God's way rather than her own. She had missed the hope of God's power that routed Israel's enemies and brought the people of God into the promised land. Her personal conquest to gain victory was the rampart that kept God at bay.

When her hope turned from herself and "her" program and turned instead to hope in God, God became present in a new way. It was no longer her fighting against "them," whoever "they" were. The rest of the church was struggling to do God's will even as Michelle was, with the limited resources available. Here were other thirsty souls, like herself, disturbed souls who journeyed to the waters to be soothed and cleansed. Here was help that indeed her soul could trust.

> Why are you downcast, O my soul?
>   Why so disturbed within me?
> Put your hope in God,
>   for I will yet praise him,
>   my Savior and my God.

INTIMACY

For you created my inmost being;
you knit me together in my mother's womb.
I praise you because I am fearfully and wonderfully made;
your works are wonderful,
I know that full well. (Psalm 139:13-14)

A pastor who specializes in counseling made the interesting statement that one of the most pervasive characteristics of those whom he counsels is fear of loneliness. There is the fear that if other people in their lives—even those who know them most intimately—find out who they really are, they will suddenly abandon them. There is the fear that people will not accept them for who they are as individuals.

A young man shared how he was afraid to be himself while dating in high school. He liked a girl, but didn't think she would accept him for the shy, introspective person he was. And so, he acted in concert with her expectations. While he wanted more than ever to be true to himself, the deeper he got into the relationship, the more afraid he became that exposing who he really was would end the relationship. He felt trapped, and more and more distant from her than ever.

So he couched his feelings. He camouflaged his thoughts. He packed away his emotions in a box labeled "Do not open." He looked to mimic others rather than looking inside to find himself. Try as he might, he didn't feel close to his girlfriend as long as he was being dishonest with himself. It was a painful lesson that convinced him he couldn't be satisfied in another relationship with himself or others until he was totally honest.

It could be that most of us are like that in some respect, even with God. We are tempted to put on a façade. We are lured into painting over our humanness with a pure Christian latex exterior that covers anything sinful from the eyes of God or the world. We hide our feelings; we pretend everything is going just fine; we say all the right words on Sunday in order not to push God away. But doing so only makes us feel farther away than ever from the One who already knows us inside and out. We struggle to have an intimate relationship with God even as we keep God at an arm's distance.

We are not called to be phony Christians, nor are we called to be perfect people. We are called to be God's children. We are welcomed with open arms, arms stretched wide on the cross so that we might have life. We are called simply to approach God and be with God and to let God love us as God desires.

Have you let God get close to you by sharing your fears, joys, insecurities, and sin? God already knows your getting up and lying down, as well as your deepest thoughts. You have been chosen, just as you are, to love God and to be loved by God, inside and out.

JOY

Do not grieve, for the joy of the Lord is your strength. (Nehemiah 8:10)

E merson once observed that, "Most of the shadows in this life are caused by standing in our own sunshine." His thought is one of thousands as to why the quality of joy is sometimes missing from life. We all seek joy, happiness, and contentment. Where do they hide during our dark and cloudy days?

The Bible tells us that the joy of the Christian is found in Jesus. In John 15:11 Jesus says, "These things I have spoken unto you, that my joy might remain in you, and that your joy might be full." That's a promise. Jesus said we could have joy like his own. It's a free gift.

But like any gift or talent, we need to cultivate joy in order for it to add zest to our life and the lives of others. "Joy is one of the great Christian virtues," observed Lucius C. Porter. "An uplifting part of the joy Jesus brought to His disciples was the joy of sharing. And sharing is the essence of the Christian gospel." It is clear that joy is not something to keep to ourselves.

Galatians 5:22 gives us another source of joy. It says "The fruit of the Spirit is love, joy and faith." Joy is not something we have, but rather something given to us and created in us by the Spirit. John 16:24 adds that all we need to do is, "Ask and you will receive, and your joy will be complete." God wants us to have joy and gives it to those who ask for it in prayer.

One of our founding fathers, Patrick Henry, knew the source of true joy. When he made his last will and testament he wrote, "I have now disposed of all my property to my family. My most cherished possession I wish I could leave with you is my faith in Jesus Christ, for with Him and nothing else you can be happy, but without Him and with all else you'll never be happy."

Joy is not to be found in the things of this world. We'll never find it there. We'll only have joy when we look inside and feel the spirit of Christ within us. Jesus is our help, our salvation, and our joy.

KNOWLEDGE

For God, who said, "Let light shine out of darkness," made his light shine in our hearts to give us the light of the knowledge of the glory of God in the face of Christ.

But we have this treasure in jars of clay to show that this all-surpassing power is from God and not from us. (2 Corinthians 4:6-7)

The adult volunteer was excited about the opportunity to attend a national ecumenical conference for youth workers. When he got there, speakers from around the country and from a variety of denominations addressed issues from teen relationships to spirituality to organizing youth ministry to teaching Sunday school classes for teens. The talks were biblically based and well received. People were excited about what they had heard and were eager to get back to their churches to begin work.

In the midst of all the excitement, however, the volunteer felt frustrated and perplexed. He had enjoyed all the speakers and had heard words that rang true from his experience, but who was right? The speakers had opposing messages; even those with whom he talked disagreed about biblical truths and about God's nature and human responsibility. How could all of these people, all well-intentioned Christians, be right and yet disagree with one another? Who knew the real truth? Shouldn't somebody be able to answer all the tough questions?

We are surrounded by different truths and people who want to tell us what we should or shouldn't know. It's as easy as watching different TV evangelists on Sunday morning. Each one reads and preaches from the same Bible, yet the messages are very different. On what do we base our knowledge? How can we learn more about God and our faith?

Ultimately, it is God who gives us knowledge. God indeed is truth, and it is God who gives us the truth through the Holy Spirit. We as humans are simply fragile containers that try to hold this truth and knowledge as best we can. We are earthen vessels, jars of clay, made from earthly elements and water. Our ways of knowing, without God, are limited to this earth. Our truth, without God, is limited to our own perception. God gives us knowledge as we open ourselves to God's workings. God has "made his light shine in our hearts to give us the light of the knowledge of the glory of God in the face of Christ."

We need not confine God by trying to understand all there is to know about the divine. Trying to confine God or knowledge about God is like trying to confine jello. The more we squeeze, the more it slips out of our grasp. Rather, we need to be open to God, to let the light shine into our hearts and be ready for God to surprise us. Yes, we are jars of clay, earthen vessels, fragile creatures quick to find life and knowledge by ourselves. However, without the master craftsman, the One who gives us the light of the knowledge of God's glory, we'll simply stay in the dark.

LIMITS

Then Job replied to the LORD:
"I know that you can do all things;
*   no plan of yours can be thwarted.*
Surely I spoke of things I did not understand,
*   things too wonderful for me to know." (Job 42:1-2, 3b)*

Dear God: A woman was telling a preacher the other day that we should use your name whenever we had the chance to prove to people that we were not secretly a bunch of secular humanists. Remember her? Yea, that one. Her comments made some people very upset, talking as though your name were a secret formula for success.

It used to be that people refused to even mention your name for the longest time, simply because it was too holy and too wonderful to be bound by a few itty bitty letters. Now people grab it like a tiger by the tail and swear they've got control of you. Or they use your name like a genie in a bottle, as if uttering it gave them all the power in the world and put everybody else at their command.

People must at least wonder, and it must make you a bit perturbed (not to let anyone put thoughts or feelings inside the Almighty), when people box you up and package you like a product on the market. How can people try to fit such limitlessness into a few pounds of brain (and darned if we all don't do the same thing!).

Well, anyway, help us try to keep you big in our own minds. Tell us to move over. Shake us up and turn us upside down and tell us we need to make room for someone other than ourselves. Tell us not to ask why or how or if it will be enough. Just tell us to move over and make room. Open up our minds and our souls and our hearts and our wills and our complacency and our desires and our careful planning and our best-laid intentions and just move us aside, shoo us on over! Because you're too big and too wonderful and too powerful and too personal and too loving and too forgiving to be bound and tied by any strings of the imagination, especially ours. Amen

LISTENING

*Many, O L*ord *my God,*
  are the wonders you have done.
Sacrifice and offering you did not desire,
  but my ears you have pierced. (Psalm 40:5a, 6a)

You know the scenario well enough. You've just heard some great news, news you can't wait to share with someone special. You wait for just the right moment to start pouring out all the wonderful details. But then you glance at your listener, only to find their eyes off in the distance and their minds as far south as the Florida Keys.

It may seem for many of us that we do the same thing to God in our time of prayer. God's wonders are before us, yet our minds are off in the distance, scurrying behind the noise of tasks and upcoming responsibilities and personal concerns. Our impatience for a divine reply can often cause us to fill the silence with inner chatter and requests. It's hard for us to listen to God and let God's presence surround us.

A woman was looking for her first new car. When the salesman asked what she was looking for, the young adult replied, "Something like a small station wagon—good gas mileage, but something versatile that can also haul a few things."

Out on the lot the salesman showed her a few "specials," cars the salesman obviously liked and thought were good buys. "It's too bad you're not looking for something like this," the salesman said.

It was too bad. Not only did the young woman leave the lot empty-handed, but the salesman went home without a sale. He didn't listen for what the woman wanted in a car, and the potential car buyer wasn't going to waste her energy trying to convince the salesman that their needs were obviously different. So the young woman went to another lot where they showed her a small station wagon that fit the bill perfectly. She drove home with a new car.

When we put on our car salesman clothes and meet with God, we leave empty-handed. When we try to sell God the things we want rather than what God wants, we miss an opportunity. When we spend time trying to convince God what is best for our lives rather than listening to what God desires for us, we have closed another door from which God might enter.

It's hard to listen, to wait in the silence and hear nothing but the echoes of our thoughts. It's hard to wait for God to act and to speak so that we might hear. But God is speaking all the time, even as the Spirit is moving and hovering over the troubled waters in our lives. Oh yes, God speaks; we simply need to listen.

May we dare, like the psalmist, to let God pierce our ears so that we might listen and hear the movement and power of the Spirit.

LOVE*

A new command I give you: Love one another. As I have loved you, so you must love one another. (John 13:34)

In David Dunn's book, *Try Giving Yourself Away*, the author shows how acts of kindness and appreciation can transform the lives of others while bringing increased personal satisfaction and happiness. Dunn cites dozens of examples of how a kind word or an act of compassion can change lives. He notes how giving is much more satisfying than getting and how simple it is to put giving into daily practice.

What Dunn promotes is love in action. It is the same powerful concept that Jesus talks about in John's Gospel. Jesus told his disciples, "A new command I give you: Love one another. As I have loved you, so you must love one another." Jesus then said, "By this all men will know that you are my disciples" (John 13:34-35). Jesus knew that the only way to change the world and to transform lives was to put love into practice—in other words, to give love away.

So often we long for love and appreciation from others. Yet, it is seldom we realize that what we receive in this life we obtain from giving. There is a hunger for a love that satisfies. We look for love in relationships with family, friends, and spouses. However, our search for love can be elusive. We are looking for something that is already inside of us. What we need to do to find love is to release love. This is strange, but true.

Jesus called love a new commandment. He ranked love in importance with God's call not to kill or steal. Christ told his disciples that demonstrating love to others and one another was proof of their relationship with him. He wanted love to be a mark of identification then, and he still wants that for us today. As his disciples, our displays of love help others to know us, and they will want to learn about our source of love.

It isn't always easy to give love away. Giving love away is risky. We risk rejection and make ourselves vulnerable to being hurt. It takes emotional effort and energy. Giving away love means we take away a focus on ourselves and give attention to another. We give a part of ourselves with no guarantees for anything in return.

God gave us an abundance of love. The more we give, the more others will know we belong to God.

*This devotion originally appeared in *Exploring the Yearly Lectionary, Series C* (Minneapolis: Augsburg Fortress, 1991), p. 63. Copyright © by Augsburg Fortress. Reprinted by permission.

MEMORIES

Remember how the LORD your God led you all the way in the desert these forty years. . . . But remember the LORD your God, for it is he who gives you the ability to produce wealth, and so confirms his covenant, which he swore to your forefathers, as it is today. (Deuteronomy 8:2, 18)

The older couple recalled their time on the farm shortly after they were married. They raised chickens, milked a few cows, and had a small garden to provide for themselves. It was an extremely difficult time. The husband related how his wife had been out in the barn, milking a cow on a one-legged stool. She was pregnant, but still kept busy with the daily chores so that they might make ends meet. The cow kicked her unexpectedly in the abdomen, knocking her backwards. She started bleeding terribly, and passed out cold as the husband rushed over to her. "It was like dragging a board into the house," he remembered. The husband called the doctor, who came over immediately. The doctor was able to stop the bleeding and stitched her up. She recovered shortly thereafter, and later gave birth to a healthy boy.

It's a terrible story in one sense, but it's also a story of thanks. In the midst of the bad are memories of the good. Although things were tough, God provided for this couple. Remembering God's help in the worst of times allowed them to give thanks for the present and to look forward to God's care in the future.

The memories of past events assure us that God will take care of our needs in the future as well. In fact, it's precisely because God has proved trustworthy in the past that we can be certain that God will be with us tomorrow and the next day. God has not simply created us and let us go our own way to fend for ourselves. God created us and renews us daily, mindful of the covenant made in the past. It's the past that gives us hope for the future; the past assures us that the God of Abraham and Sarah and Moses is the same God that calls and cares for us today in our own times of joy and pain. God's work of salvation doesn't end, but continues into the future.

Memories remind us of how God has worked in our lives bringing good out of bad situations. It is in those memories, both great and small, in which we catch a glimpse of the divine in our lives. And so we remember, we cherish the memories. For God is our God, now and forever.

MIRACLES

"Where is your faith?" he asked his disciples.
In fear and amazement they asked one another, "Who is this? He com-
mands even the winds and the water, and they obey him." (Luke 8:25)

The new mother was filling out the baby book shortly after she had arrived home from the hospital with the family's first baby boy. "What were your thoughts when Andrew was born?" she yelled down the stairs.

The husband didn't have to think long. It was the head. At first it stubbornly resisted showing itself to the outside world, moving like a wave forward and back with each contraction. But when at last it could not retreat back into the safety of the womb, it finally appeared massive and demanding. What a big head, he remembered himself thinking, only to gasp involuntarily as the other half of the noggin slid out.

Who said miracles don't happen anymore? These new parents didn't believe it for a minute! Not because they were Christians or theologians, but because they were parents. After all, who can explain *why* (not how) children are created through a relationship of man and woman? Who can explain the instinctive caring and nurturing of the mother? Let science and technology try—even they cannot prove the unprovable. And who said anything about what is spiritual? Science has enough limits of verifiability even in the scientific world—what do they know about the spiritual?

So what about miracles? Is it that they don't occur, or could it be that we are simply not open to them occurring? Could it be we're so convinced they're impossible that when a miracle looks us in the eye we miss it? Could it be we've overlooked the opportunities and excitement of how God surprises us simply because we have kept our eyes closed?

Miracles do happen. They happen all the time. We simply need to listen to those around us to see how God is working wonders in our world. For instance, a youth shared what happened to him when his favorite grandfather died. He felt angry, confused, and hurt. He related how he pondered life's meaning, wondering if it was worth living any more. But in the despair a miracle happened. He came to church, where a group of adults accepted him and loved him. "If it wasn't for the church," he said, "I'm not sure I could have handled Grandpa's death. Now I want to do something for those people who helped me. I want to give something back to others."

Who said miracles don't happen anymore? Keep your eyes open. You may be in for the surprise of your life.

PEACE

"Peace I leave with you; my peace I give you. I do not give to you as the world gives." (John 14:27)

There is a poster with a picture of a storm-swollen sea, surrounded by angry-looking clouds pouring out their wet misery. Whitecaps are crashing and fuming against the rocks in the foreground. Tucked in the corner, however, is a secluded bay quite at peace, protected by an overhanging rock. The caption reads, "Peace is not found outside the storm, but in the midst of it."

What is your first reaction when a tempest assails you, when the paper work starts devouring your desk, when committee meetings swallow you whole, when Murphy's law is the only law in your universe? Is your reaction to create more diversions, or to face the tumult and place its fury into the hands of Jesus, the Prince of Peace? Surprisingly, our peace may not always be found away from life's furies, but often in the very midst of them.

Our peace, therefore, may be found in the storm of peer pressure, when we decide that following God is more appropriate than group consensus. Our peace may be discovered in the avalanche of responsibilities when we are forced to admit we cannot do everything on our own because of human limitations. Peace may surface in the tremors of physical or psychological pain, when suddenly the reality of our finite existence is soothed by the immensity of our eternal life with God. Our peace might be uncovered in the hurt of a broken relationship, when we find out that God accepts us just as we are.

It is in these stormy times that God is able to speak to us, and we are able to listen. It is in these moments that we find the comfort of God's unconditional love, as we hear God's promise of never leaving or forsaking us.

Peace in the midst of the storm. Not the kind of peace earned by human endeavor, but the lasting peace given us as we weather the gales of life with our gracious Lord and Savior.

PERFECTION

It is God who arms me with strength
and makes my way perfect. (Psalm 18:32)

Although we may not view Ben Franklin as a spiritual leader, he was keenly aware of his relationship with God. The man we know as a printer, scientist, politician, inventor, and author knew he was blessed by God with many talents and sought to make the most of them.

But while he accomplished many things, mere accomplishments were not enough. Franklin longed to be perfect. "I conceived the bold project of arriving at moral perfection," he wrote. "I wished to live without committing any fault at any time; I would conquer all that natural inclination, custom, or company might lead me into."

Like most of us, Franklin knew, or thought he knew, the difference between right and wrong. He thought it would be easy to avoid wrong and do what was right. "But I soon found," he wrote later, "that I had undertaken a task of more difficulty than I had imagined. While my care was employed in guarding against one fault, I was often surprised by another."

So Franklin changed his tactics. He listed what he considered to be the twelve most important virtues. Each night he reviewed his list and placed a black mark by any failings. When this didn't work he decided to concentrate on adhering to one virtue each week, doing his best on the other twelve. Franklin did this for several years. "I never arrived at perfection," he later revealed, "but fell far short of it. Yet I was a better and happier man. . . . Only some device as this will ensure steady progress toward virtue" (*Autobiography of Ben Franklin* [New York: Dodd, Mead & Company, 1963], pp. 88-97).

Just as Ben Franklin wished he could be a better person, we, too, strive to be more like Christ, God's example of human perfection. And like Franklin, we make some progress, but never enough. We are not perfect. We are God's people in an imperfect world.

However, the good news of the gospel proclaims forgiveness for our imperfections and the love of God just the way we are. We have the tool of prayer for obtaining God's help in our quest, along with the ability to learn from our mistakes as the Holy Spirit works in and through us. "Every good and perfect gift is from above, coming down from the Father of the heavenly lights" (James 1:17).

POSSIBILITIES

Knock and the door will be opened to you. (Luke 11:9b)

During the early 1900s, Beatrice Kay was a rising young star in vaudeville. She had a beautiful voice and specialized in love songs. Eventually she joined the Princetown Follies and her fame increased. Then she had a severe attack of laryngitis.

Her doctor advised her not to talk or sing for an entire year. After obeying her doctor's orders for a period of time, she attempted to talk and her voice returned. But it was a new voice containing a slight rasp that was completely unsuited to performing love songs.

Although her voice had changed, her determination to become a major star was as strong as ever. Rather than giving up her dream, Miss Kay created a new style and character to match her new voice. By capitalizing on her "defect," she became a popular singing comedian and drew laughter from old beer hall ballads of the 1890s. Her records sold millions through the 1950s.

Beatrice Kay found, as others have, that every door opens to something. What appears to be a closed door or an impossible situation doesn't necessarily mean anything. God says, knock and it shall be opened to you.

Through our experiences in life, God shows us that having faith and simply attempting the "impossible" is life changing. If we only begin, through faith, to tackle a challenge, God makes it possible for us to accomplish our dreams. The process strengthens our faith in our abilities and in God as we knock on doors. And what we learn is that God always provides a way.

It's been said that when you limit what you will do, you limit what you can do. The same can be applied to congregations, churches, and ministries. It is so easy to create our own limits in doing God's work. We don't have the time. We don't have the experience. We don't have it in the budget. We don't have the necessary talent or ability. Situations seem impossible because we don't open our thinking to the possible.

The next time you are faced with an impossible situation, remember that God invites us to knock on doors. God will provide a way, a way that may well be more fruitful and exciting than what we could ever imagine.

PRAYER

Do not be anxious about anything, but in everything, by prayer and petition, with thanksgiving, present your requests to God. And the peace of God, which transcends all understanding, will guard your hearts and your minds in Christ Jesus. (Philippians 4:6-7)

How much time should we spend in prayer? It has been shown that the average church-goer spends about four minutes a day in prayer. That's not much considering that when asked, most Christians say they do believe in the power of prayer. Why don't we pray more?

There are perhaps many reasons. We may be in too much of a rush in the morning and at night, or perhaps we are too tired. But often it is more than that. It can stem from a lack of faith, not knowing how to pray, and maybe even doubting that prayer accomplishes anything. Most of us want to pray and have a strong prayer life, but when it comes down to it, we fall short of our goal.

It is said that a former president once observed:

> Personal prayer, it seems to me, is one of the simple necessities of life, as basic to the individual as sunshine, food and water—and at times of course, more so. By prayer I believe we mean an effort to get in touch with the Infinite. We know that our prayers are imperfect. Of course they are. We are imperfect human beings. A thousand experiences have convinced me beyond room of doubt that prayer multiplies the strength of the individual and brings within the scope of his or her capabilities almost any conceivable objective.

Just as this former president knew the power of prayer, we also can become better at tapping this source of personal and spiritual strength. Jesus has shown us how to pray as he showed his disciples. God desires that we pray with thanksgiving and that we be honest about our thoughts, word, and deeds. Prayer is a unique privilege we share as children of God. It is our communication with our Father that shows our desire to cooperate with God's will.

Prayer does influence God. In James 5:16-18, we read:

Therefore confess your sins to each other and pray for each other so that you may be healed. The prayer of a righteous man is powerful and effective.

Elijah was a man just like us. He prayed earnestly that it would not rain, and it did not rain on the land for three and a half years. Again he prayed, and the heavens gave rain, and the earth produced its crops.

Perhaps it is time to take a new look at what prayer means to us. It is a means of communication, just as making a telephone call or writing a letter. We need it to be a high priority. We need to do it more often. No one ever regretted praying too much, though many regret praying too little.

There is an old German proverb that says, "When in prayer you clasp your hands, God opens his." That's the beauty of making our requests known to God.

QUIET

Then, because so many people were coming and going that they did not even have a chance to eat, [Jesus] said to them, "Come with me by yourselves to a quiet place and get some rest." (Mark 6:31)

The story is told of a mother who telephoned to have a taxi sent to her home. When the cab arrived, the woman brought out three young children and instructed them to get into the cab. She told the driver to put the meter on and that she would return in a few minutes. After twenty minutes of waiting, the cab driver did not know what to do. But then the woman appeared and asked what she owed. Puzzled, the driver asked if she was going anyplace. She replied, "No, I had to make a long distance telephone call and I needed some peace and quiet."

Peace and quiet. That's what all of us need from time to time. We need a time of rest from daily pressures and responsibilities. We need an escape from telephones, interruptions, and noise. For many people it seems peace and quiet are a luxury—an infrequent respite from a frantic world.

But just because this world moves at a frantic pace, it doesn't mean we must do the same. That's easier said than done, however, as we get caught up in meetings, appointments, parties, work, family obligations, and the stress of life. We sometimes forget about God as we struggle to get things done in time. And in the end, we wonder where all our time went.

So how do we find quiet time? Just as Jesus told his disciples, "Come with me by yourselves to a quiet place and get some rest," we, too, need to do the same. Perhaps we need to reserve some quiet time first thing in the morning so we can focus our lives and meditate on God's word. Or maybe we need to take a break at noon for more than just lunch and experience some food for the soul. God has given us imagination and time. It is up to us to find our own quiet moments.

We can certainly tithe our time, giving God the first fruits (first minutes) of a new day. Quiet time spent with God can be our best moments as we offer ourselves and time to God for direction and guidance. Both our bodies and spirits need the peace that only God can provide.

So come away by yourself and be refreshed by the love, encouragement, and power that comes from no other source. When you do, God will provide strength for the day and the peace and quiet you need, no matter how busy you are.

RELATIONSHIPS

Live a life of love, just as Christ loved us. (Ephesians 5:2)

A church hired a man to paint the steeple of their church. The painter began at the top and about halfway down realized he would run short of paint. Not wanting to climb all the way down to the ground to get more paint, he added some thinner and continued painting.

Further down, he ran low again so he added more thinner. No sooner had he finished the job, than it began to rain. As he watched all the paint being washed off the steeple, he looked to the heavens and shouted, "God, what should I do?" A voice from above answered, "Repaint, repaint, and thin no more."

Taking shortcuts can ruin our finest intentions. Like the painter, we, too, sometimes add "thinner" and are later surprised to find we have been washed out. This is especially true in relationships when we cut back on time spent together in order to devote extra effort to work, a hobby, or a cause. As a result, we get spread too thin, and the paint that held the relationship together begins to peel.

Relationships are a blessing from God, and like any blessing they can be easily taken for granted, until the blessing disappears. God has given us the gift of time to nurture these relationships, but often misguided priorities get in the way. We are given all the time we need to enjoy friendships. What we sometimes lack is the common sense to treasure and enjoy them.

Relationships, especially those most important to us, need a generous amount of togetherness and conversation in order to remain fresh and alive. Taking a walk together, going out to dinner, making a date once a week, or even shopping together can help prevent a "wash out" and assist in keeping priorities straight.

What is a friend? F. W. Robertson defines a friend as "a person on whose fidelity you can count, whose success in life flushes your cheek with honest satisfaction, for whose honor you would answer as for your own, given to you by circumstances over which you have no control, a gift from God." How easy it is at times to forget about the gift and the Giver!

God has given us special people who add joy and fulfillment to our life. Take pleasure in them. Thank God for them. Grow closer to them. Because just like a quality paint job, relationships that are given constant maintenance last a long, long time.

RESOURCES

His divine power has given us everything we need. (2 Peter 1:3a)

$\mathbf{M}$any decades ago, a small town newspaper editor was sitting at his desk one night trying to write an editorial. After struggling with the words for about an hour, he paused from his labor and happened to glance down at the floor. What he saw became the subject of his weekly message.

The editor observed a large black beetle lying on its back, vainly trying to turn over. The editor watched as it struggled with its legs sticking straight up in the air trying to grasp something so it could turn over. The beetle worked until it was exhausted and then lay there motionless as if dead. It might have died there if the editor hadn't given it a boost.

The incident made an impression on the editor. He found it interesting that the poor creature had evidently forgotten that under its shell it had strong wings it could have used to extricate itself from its perilous position.

Later that night he wrote, "Is mankind any wiser than the beetle? Some are, but many are just as helpless when 'placed on their back.' They fret and fume and paw the air and say they never had a chance, waiting for someone to come along and place them 'on their feet' again. They forget to use the resources they have to help them out in times of trouble" (*Pelican Rapids Press,* Pelican Rapids, Minnesota, 1913).

God has also furnished us with "wings" to help us in our day-to-day struggles. Our resources include prayer, patience, humor, friends, creativity, faith, and determination, all of which can get us out of difficult situations. That's quite an impressive list when you look at it. And what's really amazing is that the list is endless. We have more resources than most of us realize or will ever use.

We do have everything we need. It is all part of God's amazing grace and love. As we have been blessed with resources, we also become God's resources, serving his Church with our many talents and gifts.

Have you taken a personal inventory lately of all your resources and talents? How about the resources available through the people in your church? God has given us resources for the purpose of doing God's work on earth, helping others, and furthering God's kingdom. Let's respond in faith to all God has provided.

REST

By the seventh day God had finished the work he had been doing; so on the seventh day he rested from all his work. (Genesis 2:2)

Herbert Goldstein writes, "The Sabbath is what you make of it—a holy day, a holiday, a rest day, a sports day, or if you're not smart, another work day."

Hectic schedules seem to be a way of life now, and are as common for the grade schooler as they are for adults. It's not unusual to find youth in junior high already burned out from overinvolvement in sports, school, or hobbies. Spare moments are filled with activity, and even our weekends become events from which we need to recover.

A woman talked about her memorable weekends of family camping. On Thursday evening the family got busy packing up the car. Friday evening she would rush home after work to cook a quick meal and get the family ready. After swallowing their meals whole, she would pile the kids into the car and fight traffic for several hours to their favorite campsite. Once they arrived, they raced the waning hours of light to set up camp before the sun went down.

Saturday was their day to relax. Sunday afternoon was packing up and fighting the traffic back home. Sunday night was spent cleaning and washing clothes. Monday was spent wondering where the weekend had gone.

It may be helpful to think of recreation as a means of re-creation. It's a time for us to pause, to relax, to think, to recharge our drained batteries. It's a time to be refreshed, rather than a time of creating more things to do.

It's notable that even God took a break from the work of creation with a day of rest. Whether God needed it or not might be up for grabs, but it was a pattern that started the Sabbath, a day when people stopped their work and spent time with God and their families.

Relaxing doesn't come easily, however, even as Christians. Our puritanical work ethics cringe at the thought of slowing down. A challenge to mind our tempo may appear to be out of touch with reality in such a fast paced world. Even with the best intentions, we may neglect the invitation to rest.

But as Christians, we need to become better "resters." Not because it is a luxury, but because it is a necessity. It's a time when God gives us the special gifts of wonder and enjoyment and contentment that helps us, in turn, complete the other tasks that fill our schedules. It's a time for renewal, whether it lasts a few minutes or a few hours, whether it's enjoying the creation or finding respite in the blessings of God's mercy and love.

Rest and relaxation are also ways of putting things into perspective. It's a way of saying that nothing is so important that it can't be interrupted by a break. It's a way of you controlling your schedule rather than your schedule controlling you.

Being intentional about relaxing isn't only enjoyable, it's healthy and efficient as well. As you complete the tasks God has given you, keep in mind the Yugoslav proverb that says, "A good rest is half the work."

STRENGTH

My flesh and my heart may fail,
but God is the strength of my heart
and my portion forever. (Psalm 73:26)

On November 23, 1963, the day after President Kennedy was killed, one of the top comics in the nation was scheduled to perform before a sold-out crowd. He didn't feel like making people laugh that night. The crowd probably didn't feel like laughing either, he thought. Here is how he handled the situation:

"Ladies and gentlemen," he began. "There is no sense pretending we do not know what happened yesterday. We know. But one of these days—today, Tuesday, or a week from Tuesday—one of these days we're going to have to go back to work, remembering we are still alive.

"Tonight is my night to go back to work. If you were in the business of making people laugh, like I am, you might feel like I do and want to wait a month or year before trying again. But I'm here tonight and you're here tonight.

"Once I was lucky enough to be asked to do a show for President Kennedy. He had a warm and beautiful sense of humor. I'd like to do for you exactly the same show I did for him. You don't have to laugh. I don't expect you to" (Alan Sherman, *A Gift of Laughter* [New York: Atheneum Publishers, 1965], p. 297).

What happened that night might remind you of the phrase, "The show must go on." And so it is with life. Life must go on even in the face of loss and emptiness. As Christians living in a troubled world, we are called by God to persevere. We may not feel like it, we may not have the energy, but God calls us to serve others in the most trying of times.

It is God who empowers us to serve. He establishes and strengthens us in faith for the work we are called to do. It is in these dark hours that we can embrace the love and power of God which has sustained us before.

God gives us strength through prayer, through the Spirit, and through the love of others. We can go on, we can serve, and we can live because Christ lives. He has promised us that there is nothing we can't handle as long as we look to him as our source of strength.

What can we do when we need strength? We can join with the psalmist saying:

God is our refuge and strength,
   an ever present help in trouble.
Therefore we will not fear, though the earth give way
   and the mountains fall into the heart of the sea,
though its waters roar and foam
   and the mountains quake with their surging. (Psalm 46:1-3)

SUPPORT

When you walk through the fire,
  you will not be burned;
  the flames will not set you ablaze.
For I am the LORD, your God,
  the Holy One of Israel, your Savior. (Isaiah 43:2b-3a)

And we urge you, brothers, warn those
  who are idle, encourage the timid,
  help the weak, be patient with everyone. (1 Thessalonians 5:14)

Several years ago during a fall retreat at a church camp, a group of five young adults was scheduled by its leader to experience "the ropes course." It was a series of situations where accomplishment seemed impossible.

At one point the group was faced with climbing over a long log suspended nine feet in the air, looking like a football goalpost. Some in the group believed only ropes or a ladder would make this task possible. These resources were not available, however. All they had were one another.

Together, the young adults formed a "human pyramid" and each one was able to climb up, grab on to the log, and get on top. That was just the half of it, however. Each one had to get down from the log, a nine-foot drop to the ground. Trust was the only alternative to bodily injury. Eventually, each one let go and fell into the arms of those on the ground. A team effort made the impossible possible.

People need people in order to accomplish dreams and goals. It's part of God's design that we should support others, work as a team, and that others should support us. To alter this balance is to risk a fall.

It is wonderful how God supports us in our climb up and over those obstacles that get in our way. In many cases it is through people who enter our lives. They touch us, care for us, and listen. God also provides prayer as a support system. We have the opportunity to share with other Christians, to pray together and study God's word as a member of God's team.

Life isn't always easy. It is often a struggle, but we are not alone as we face tomorrow's challenges. Whether we win or lose, God never stops loving us. That's support. It is the same kind of support God encourages us to give freely to others.

THANKSGIVING

Great is the LORD and most worthy of praise;
his greatness no one can fathom. (Psalm 145:3)

Today is a day of thanksgiving. So was yesterday. And tomorrow will also be a time of giving thanks. Thanksgiving is a daily attitude and action for all those who believe in the goodness of God and share a need to praise God for all he has done.

For Christians, thanksgiving is a way of life. We live with thanksgiving. We give thanks to our God who has given us life, who sustains us and gives us a personal relationship with him as a child of God. Thanksgiving is born from the grace of God.

What are you thankful for today? There is so much when we consider how much we have been given. We often thank God for the necessities of life—food, clothing, home, family, work, health, and friends. We thank God for freedom, the ability to make our own choices and do what we want. And then there are the little things, what we should actually call the big things in life. They include the love of others, the beauty of the earth, laughter, kindness, honesty, truth, and all those qualities that add value to our days. We owe God a debt of gratitude for his many gifts and blessings.

Yet how often we are ungrateful to God. Life is full of situations that irritate and annoy, like the driver who is not courteous and the customer who is rude and demanding. There are no thanks in our hearts for many of life's frustrations. It is in these moments we need to remember what's really important.

Thanksgiving stems from our personal relationship with Jesus Christ, who has given us unconditional love, the promise of eternal life, and countless blessings. God loves us whether we are grateful or not. It is this loving God who sees inside our ungracious hearts and gradually removes our blinders so we eventually see our blessings more clearly. Our complaints and discontent are always temporary. What causes unhappiness today is quickly forgotten, thanks to the blessings of tomorrow.

Even with all its difficulties, it is still a wonderful life. It is often just our attitude that needs adjusting when it comes to appreciating all we have, all we are, and all we can be through God in Jesus Christ.

Tonight, before you go to bed, include in your prayer of thanks the people gathered together with you now or those that gather around you on a daily basis. The love, commitment, and fellowship of others is a blessing we experience day after day. God cares for people through people. It is one of many reasons to give God the praise, thanks, and glory he deserves.

TIME

Satisfy us in the morning with your unfailing love,
that we may sing for joy and be glad all our days. (Psalm 90:14)

A man shared a lesson in geology he had a few years ago that really made him feel uncomfortable—it's called an earthquake.

Luckily, there weren't any gory details to share. His trip to San Francisco was rather uneventful, except for the earth's fifteen-second burp that ripped up a couple hundred miles of California real estate. If he had been on a ride at the State Fair rather than in a large convention room that tossed fifty people to and fro, he said he wouldn't have given it a second thought. That is, until he got outside and watched a three-story section of the Amfac Hotel teeter back and forth, finally falling into the glass-enclosed lobby seventy-five feet below.

It was the worst quake in San Francisco since 1906. Some commented about respect for mother nature. Others wondered why God had sent judgment to what they thought was a wicked city. The man could only think how fleeting and precarious the gift of life could be. What epitaph would his deeds and actions have inscribed had he been buried in death, just one hundred yards from where he presently stood? Would he have been remembered as more than a statistic?

It wasn't the promise of eternal life that blanketed him after the shock, but rather the tenuousness of life itself. What would he hear as he stood in the midst of his Master? Would it be, "Well done, my good and faithful servant"?

Though we have a future promise, our hope is imminent and our call to serve immediate. God's call is for today. The kingdom of God, though not yet fully realized, is in our midst, and like it or not, we have a part in it. It is ours. We are God's arms and legs, helping to bring the final hope to fruition even as we wait for divine completion. Waiting for tomorrow may be a missed opportunity, both for you and the kingdom.

TIMING

You see, at just the right time, when we were still powerless, Christ died for the ungodly. But God demonstrates his own love for us in this: While we were still sinners, Christ died for us. (Romans 5:6, 8)

The two junior high friends would spend their Saturday nights gathered around an old radio. They would wait, with watches in hand, for the electronic beeps that emitted from an atomic clock in Colorado. At the sound of the beeps they could set their watches to the precise time within a millionth of a second. It was a grand day when each of them received their first quartz time pieces in high school, watches guaranteed to be accurate within a second a month. Timing was important for them.

With all the hype and energy we use to orient ourselves around the concept of the right time, it should not be surprising that timing creeps into our lives of faith as well. We wait for the best time to join a church, the right time to believe, the appropriate time to get involved. We postpone making Christian commitments until we are better people or more ready to accept the challenge.

In his Letter to the Romans, Paul states that Christ died for us at the right time. Christ died for us when we were still weak, when we were still sinners. To us, that might not seem like such a good time. Shouldn't God wait for a better opportunity?

Paul wants to make sure, however, that we realize God is working through Christ at all times. In the hiddenness, in the meaninglessness, in the desperateness of situations, God is working. Now is the time, the right time for God, even though we continue to live for ourselves or refuse God's love and mercy today and tomorrow and the next day. Now is the right time for God.

Is this the right time for God to work in your life? Are you in a period of sickness? If so, God is working. Is it a time of searching? God is out looking. Is it a time of loneliness, or despair, or death? God is working. Is it a time of unconfessed sin, or guilt, or apathy toward God or others? If so, God is working.

Just how God works might not be apparent. God's choice of time may not seem appropriate. But our assurance is that in good times and bad, God is working to heal and reconcile. For just at the right time, when we were weak and powerless, Christ died for us. While we were still sinners God reconciled us through the death of Jesus Christ. Not when we were ready; God through his mercy has made us ready. Now. Now is the time to rejoice in God through our Lord Jesus Christ, through whom we have now received reconciliation.

TRUST

Those who know your name will trust in you,
  for you, LORD, have never forsaken those who seek you. (Psalm 9:10)

Dobie Schultz worked for the railroad, laying down tracks near the Columbia Gorge. His foreman called him one day and told him to grab a chisel and a twenty-pound double jack (sledge hammer) and to follow him into a tunnel.

It was the first time Dobie had done any tunnel work, and the darkness consumed them after one hundred yards. The foreman stopped and explained they had to cut the heads off a couple of stubborn bolts. He set the chisel on the first bolt and told Dobie to set his feet, just like he had been trained to do. "Remember," the foreman said, "if you set your feet right and line up your body, you'll never miss with that sledge hammer. Okay, cut the bolt."

Dobie thought his foreman was crazy. He could barely see—what if he hit the foreman's head instead? But the order came again, "Swing."

Dobie swung, and the sledge hammer struck the head of the chisel squarely. He swung again and again and finally the bolt snapped free. The next bolt broke after only two blows.

The psalmist says that those who trust in the Lord shall not be disappointed. But we know from experience that trusting God with our lives is not an easy task. We become experts at hiding the vulnerable sides of our existence in the shadows of denial, guilt, shame, and fear.

God calls us back to set our feet right, to place our own fragile frames over the feet of God's son nailed to the cross on Calvary. And when our feet are set on Christ, we need not worry about missing. For it is then that our chains break as we swing confidently into the love and mercy of Almighty God.

TRUTH

Show me your ways, O LORD,
* teach me your paths;*
guide me in your truth and teach me,
* for you are God my Savior,*
and my hope is in you all day long. (Psalm 25:4-5).

Richard M. Nixon accepted the GOP presidential nomination in 1968 with these words: "Let us begin by committing ourselves to the truth—to see it like it is, and tell it like it is—to find the truth, to speak the truth, and to live the truth."

Though the former president's deception in Watergate might appear more dramatic than anything else we might muster up by ourselves, it is a good reminder that we cannot trust ourselves to know the truth. God is the source of truth. Our truth comes from God, and our relationship with God guides us so that we might act according to that truth. Our decisions, then, spring up from our relationship with God. Keeping God as the focal point of our decisions allows us to keep on track with the truth.

The temptation, of course, is to think that we have and know the truth, or have suddenly found God's total truth to life. And yet such assurance of knowing the truth may simply mean that we have found a truth that fits our own purposes. The truth is not something we can simply go out and find, but something that is given to us by God as we give our lives to him. The psalmist reminds us that it is the Lord that teaches us God's paths and guides us in God's truth. We need not prove who is wrong, therefore, but rather follow the One who is right.

Thomas Merton provides insight as we continue our journey for truth:

> Shall I drive evil out of my soul by wrestling with my own darkness? This is not what God has planned for me. It is sufficient to turn away from my darkness to His light. I do not have to run away from myself; it is sufficient that I find myself, not as I have made myself, by my own stupidity, but as He has made me in His wisdom and remade me in His

infinite mercy. For it is His will that my body and soul should be the Temple of His Holy Spirit, that my life should reflect the radiance of His love and my whole being repose in His peace. Then will I truly know Him, since I am in Him and He is truly in me. (*Thoughts in Solitude* [New York: Farrar, Straus & Giroux, 1956], p. 120)

UNITY

I and the Father are one. (John 10:30)

It's wonderful to have someone on your side when one person or the whole world seems to be against you. There's a closeness and a love that grows from that unity.

Jesus spoke of such a unity when he declared to the Jewish leaders that "I and the Father are one" (John 10:30). Throughout John 10, Jesus talked about his sheep and being the Good Shepherd. He said, "My sheep listen to my voice; I know them, and they follow me. I give them eternal life, and they shall never perish. No one will snatch them out of my hand" (John 10:27-28).

Just as Christ has a unity with his Father, we also have a unity with Christ as the sheep of his flock. We all have a Good Shepherd that cares for us, loves us, and protects us from all that would assail us in this world. It is a unity we share with all Christians—the rest of the flock. Christ is one with God and we are one with Christ, as are all who believe in him. That's quite a connection we can put into action through prayer and Holy Communion. It binds us all together.

For Christians, there is a sense of belonging and peace and security that comes from our relationship with God and one another. Unity provides a sense of family and it gives us strength in facing challenges today and tomorrow. The good news is that we are not in this alone. Christ has conquered death and made us his own, now and forever. He loves us more than we know and nothing can snatch us out of his hand.

It's this wonderful unity we celebrate as Christians. Although we sometimes go astray, Jesus, the Good Shepherd cares for us, feeds us, and nourishes us so we can grow spiritually and do his will.

*This devotion originally appeared in *Exploring the Yearly Lectionary, Series C* (Minneapolis: Augsburg Fortress, 1991), p. 62. Copyright © by Augsburg Fortress. Used by permission.

VISION

Where there is no vision, the people perish. (Proverbs 29:18a, KJV)

The National Air and Space Museum of the Smithsonian Institution is incredible. In the huge lobby hangs the airplane flown by Orville and Wilbur Wright on that momentous day at Kitty Hawk. Below it stands one of the capsules from the Gemini flights, used in the infancy of the space program. Charles Lindbergh's *The Spirit of St. Louis* is close at hand boasting it's first transatlantic nonstop flight. A sleek, orange plane that looks like a rocket with a few stubby wings hangs in a nearby room. Its silence betrays its astounding accomplishment of being the first plane to break the sound barrier.

People do not talk at the Smithsonian Institution, they whisper. They whisper because they are overwhelmed by the accomplishments of the brave, pioneering spirits that occupy this space. They whisper because the dreams of these creative and persistent few have become reality and convict the weakness of a doubtful public. The former pessimism and jeers of a world that said space flight was impossible lay quietly, but heavily, on the floor. In little more than half a century, history had been flipped on its ear: people could fly. Thanks to a few brave souls who dared to dream, space flight was a reality.

Dreamers are never very popular. We'd rather be realistic. But the danger of realism is that it is often an excuse to be safe. It is an excuse to be comfortable with things that neither challenge nor confront nor offer us an opportunity to grow. Being safe usually means stagnation and retreat. Like the turtle, it's hard to go anywhere when we are pulled safely within our protective shells.

We have the opportunity to dream dreams as God's people. We have the possibilities of letting the Spirit of God work powerfully in our midst. We have the abilities to turn our communities upside down with our gifts of generosity, caring, and concern. We've had plenty of time to be realistic, now we need the chance to dream. We need the chance to believe in the power of Pentecost in order to risk something to proclaim the gospel in new ways. We need the opportunity to step out in the light of the cross and take God at his word.

What is your dream of faith? What part will you add to the ongoing mission of the Church? What surprises can you offer that will challenge others to grow? Go ahead, start dreaming. It's the beginning of greater things to come.

WEALTH

For where your treasure is, there your heart will be also. (Luke 12:34)

Unlike the names of Edison, Beethoven, and Carnegie, the name of Hetty Green is not known to most people. During her life she was, however, the richest woman in the world.

Although she was wealthy, many would say the sick and homeless of her day were far richer. Because of her all-consuming desire for wealth, her name is virtually forgotten.

Hetty Green is listed in a *Guiness Book of World Records* as "the greatest miser." She kept a balance of $31 million in one bank. When she died she left an estate of $95 million.

Her consuming desire for wealth caused her to spend very little. She lived on cold oatmeal so she wouldn't have to pay for heat. Her son was forced to have his leg amputated because she refused to pay for an operation. And when she died in 1916, it was caused by apoplexy during an argument over the virtues of skim milk.

It has been said that it is our attitudes and actions that make us rich, not how much we own. Sooner or later in life, most people learn that money isn't everything. Look at the example of Hetty Green. She was certainly rich, yet she was impoverished by her attitude, values, and lack of concern for others.

Like Hetty Green, you can be poor and rich at the same time, depending on how you are living and giving. Or you can realize that wealth has nothing to do with your bank account.

As we count our riches today, maybe we need to pay closer attention to the nonfinancial wealth God has given us. And perhaps we need a reminder of how insignificant money really is in God's view of what really does matter. Money, like food, is necessary to sustain life, but we can pay too high a price for it.

God has given us many treasures. The blessings of friends, family, good health, a home, and a job should not be taken lightly. Many people lack what we sometimes take for granted. As it says in Proverbs 10:22, "The blessing of the LORD brings wealth, and he adds no trouble to it."

WISDOM

The fear of the LORD is the beginning of wisdom. (Proverbs 9:10a)

During the Great Depression, a Minneapolis woman, Minnie, borrowed $2000 to give to Laura, her best friend. Laura needed to take her husband to Arizona for special medical treatment for cancer. The husband died there, leaving the impoverished Laura with two children. She corresponded with Minnie for over four years, promising repayment, yet always asking for more. Minnie saved all Laura's letters and made duplicates of her own. Together the 280 pages of letters provide a personal look at their friendship, sacrifices, and suffering. In the end, Minnie lost her health, home, job, and friends who loaned her the $2000. She never saw Laura or her money again.

Laura was prosecuted for fraud a decade earlier by Clarence Darrow who called her "a woman who probably makes her living going up and down these lands seeking whom she may devour."

In a fragment of a letter Minnie wrote:

> I suppose I am displaying my ignorance, but it does seem like problems like this could be avoided if people behave themselves, live within their income instead of at the very edge, pay their bills, and make religion and character the center of their lives. My mother used to say, "Weakness is wickedness" and so is poor judgment, especially mine. We were all given brains and should use them in dealing with others.

As church leaders, we are called to use good judgment in our actions and in our relationships with others. It's not easy, and often we may be perplexed about what to do. But God has given us all the tools we need for utilizing good judgment. We've been blessed with brains, the ability to learn from experience, the power of prayer, and the gift of forgiveness when we make mistakes.

Because we are created in the image of God, we feel deep within us the call of God to do our best, even as we are reminded of God's love. As we strive to be faithful to that call, let's remember that God never said it would be easy. But God did say he would always be with us.